To Ameka,

MW01037316

May you be well,

Tim Desmond

SELF-COMPASSION IN PSYCHOTHERAPY

SELF-COMPASSION IN PSYCHOTHERAPY

Mindfulness-Based Practices for Healing and Transformation

TIM DESMOND

Foreword by Richard J. Davidson

W.W. Norton & Company
New York • London

For information about permission to reproduce selections from this book,
write to Permissions, W. W. Norton & Company, Inc.,
500 Fifth Avenue, New York, NY 10110

For information about special discounts for bulk purchases, please contact
W. W. Norton Special Sales at specialsales@wwnorton.com or 800-233-4830

Manufacturing by Maple Press
Production manager: Christine Critelli

Library of Congress Cataloging-in-Publication Data

Desmond, Tim, author.
Self-compassion in psychotherapy : mindfulness-based practices for
healing and transformation / Tim Desmond ; foreword by
Richard J. Davidson. — First edition.
p. ; cm.
"A Norton professional book."
Includes bibliographical references and index.
ISBN 978-0-393-71100-4 (hardcover)
I. Title.
[DNLM: 1. Mindfulness—methods. 2. Empathy. WM 425.5.C6]
RC480.5
616.89'14—dc23

2015024260

W. W. Norton & Company, Inc.
500 Fifth Avenue, New York, N.Y. 10110
www.wwnorton.com

W. W. Norton & Company Ltd.
Castle House, 75/76 Wells Street, London W1T 3QT

1 2 3 4 5 6 7 8 9 0

This book is dedicated to
Thich Nhat Hanh, Marshall Rosenberg, and Joanne Friday.

CONTENTS

ACKNOWLEDGMENTS

Anything that I understand about compassion, I owe to Thich Nhat Hanh, the monks and nuns of Plum Village, and the other spiritual teachers I have been fortunate enough to meet in my life. I can't express the depth of my gratitude to them.

Joanne Friday, my first meditation teacher, taught me that compassion is the essence of mindfulness and the foundation of fearlessness. The beautiful monks and nuns of Plum Village, especially Brothers Phap Luu, Phap Dung, Phap Tri, Phap Ho, Phap Lai and Sisters Jina, Dang Nghiem, and Hanh Nghiem are, for me, living examples that the practice of understanding and love can be applied to every moment of life. Thanks to the community of Morning Sun Mindfulness Center, especially Michael and Fern, for your support in my practice.

I have also been deeply influenced by the teachings of His Holiness the Dalai Lama XIV, Tara Brach, Jack Kornfield, Sharon Salzberg, Alan Wallace, Pema Chödrön, and their spiritual ancestors. Thanks to Marshall Rosenberg and the community of Nonviolent Communication practitioners who have helped me understand the meaning of empathy and connection. Thanks to Art Stein, my political science professor at the University of Rhode Island, who first exposed me to Thich Nhat Hanh's teachings, and his wife Clare Sartori who provided invaluable feedback during the writing of this book.

Larry Boyang has been my intellectual mentor since college, and he is the one who taught me to love science. He introduced me to many of the important ideas contained in this book, helped me develop the concept of *modular constructivism*, and is the epitome of an independent and rigorous thinker.

Thanks to the community of researchers whose tireless work has built the scientific foundation of what we know about suffering and well-being, especially Richie Davidson, Jaak Panksepp, Dan Siegel, Joseph LeDoux, Dan Kahneman, Bruce Wampold, and Richard Bentall.

Thank you so much to Richie Davidson (again) and Chris Germer for your support and encouragement. Thank you to Gary Brain, Brian Toomey, and Gavin Raders for your friendship. Thank you to Andrea Costella Dawson and Ben Yarling at W.W. Norton for your guidance in this process and for believing in me. Thank you to Tanya Bezreh and Phap Luu (again) for your feedback and help during the writing process. Thank you to my mother, Pat Desmond, who is an inspiration for me and taught me that deep, personal change is possible. Thanks to all of my clients—you've taught me more than I've taught you.

Thank you so much to Annie, my absolutely wonderful wife, whose love and support made this entire project possible. She is a brilliant editor and a bright light in the world. Thanks to my son, Finnegan, for inspiring me to be my best self.

In gratitude to parents, teachers, friends, and all beings, I bow deeply before the Three Jewels in the Ten Directions.

FOREWORD BY RICHARD J. DAVIDSON

Compassion and self-compassion lie at the very heart of well-being. For those in the helping professions, and for psychotherapists in particular, the expression of compassion and self-compassion is likely a critical constituent of being an effective therapist. This book is an extraordinarily practical and useful guide to the importance of self-compassion in psychotherapy. It is also a "how-to" manual of simple practices that can be used to kindle the development of self-compassion.

When I first met His Holiness the Dalai Lama in 1992 he challenged me, exclaiming that if I was using tools of modern neuroscience to study anxiety, depression, and fear, why couldn't I use the same tools to study kindness and compassion? At that time I did not have a very good answer to this question, but the very way His Holiness posed it awakened a calling in me to dedicate the remainder of my work life to this topic. In 2009 we established the Center for Investigating Healthy Minds at the University of Wisconsin-Madison, which has as its mission the cultivation of well-being and relief of suffering through a scientific understanding of the mind. Following this life-altering initial meeting with the Dalai Lama, compassion was among the very first topics we elected to study with the tools of modern neuroscience. And over the past 6 years we, along with a cadre of young scientific explorers, have begun for the first time to seriously study the neural and behavioral correlates of mental training to cultivate compassion.

We have learned that training as little as 30 minutes a day for 2 weeks is sufficient, in complete novices, to change the brain and induce more prosocial and altruistic behavior. These changes have been observed in rigorous, randomized, controlled trials in which we treated the compassion training in the same way other researchers might treat the evaluation of a new pharmaceutical. We have also learned from this corpus of new findings that compassion is not empathy. While compassion and empathy each activate some of the same circuits in the brain, there are important differences. Compassion activates circuits that have been associated with positive emotion and reward, while empathy does not necessarily include the activation of those circuits. Moreover, compassion leads to prosocial behavior more systematically than empathy.

The wonderful insights, vignettes, and wise teachings sprinkled throughout this book will be of great benefit to any clinician who wishes to incorporate compassion practices in his or her work. Determining the most effective strategies for consolidating these insights into enduring change remains an important task for the future. It will also remain critical to rigorously assess what exactly the benefits of self-compassion training are for therapeutic outcomes. If there are measureable, objective changes in therapeutic outcome as a consequence of the types of practices described in this volume, it will have very important implications for psychotherapy training. The increased availability of these practices and the receptivity of the field to the integration of contemplative approaches with modern psychology bode well for a more informed and integrative approach to psychotherapy in the future.

SELF-COMPASSION IN
PSYCHOTHERAPY

Chapter 1

SELF-COMPASSION

What Is It and Why Is It Useful in Therapy?

Many years ago, I was on a 3-month meditation retreat with Thich Nhat Hanh at a Buddhist monastery in the mountains outside of San Diego. I was sitting on a boulder that overlooked the ocean with one of the senior monks and asked him for advice about how to focus my meditation practice while I was there. He said, "Whenever any kind of suffering arises, even if it's minor or subtle, recognize that it is there and send it compassion." Over the next 3 months, I discovered how powerful this simple practice could be. I saw that whenever I felt anxious or insecure or lonely, just a few minutes of self-compassion produced a real change. I found that these feelings could actually be comforted, and that when I practiced like this, I could let go of whatever was bothering me and live more fully in the present moment.

In many ways that conversation has shaped the course of my life as well as my work as a psychotherapist and meditation teacher. The practice of recognizing suffering and sending it compassion is at the core of how I work with people, and I've found that this simple and direct method can be enormously effective with everyday suffering, as well as with severe depression, anxiety, and trauma. It also has the ability to generate happiness and help us pay more attention to the positive elements of life.

The purpose of this book is to give you all the tools you need to apply self-compassion practices to real-life clinical situations. We will explore how to help your clients develop self-compassion, as well as how practicing it yourself can make you a happier and more effective therapist. These two areas of focus—teaching your clients to practice self-compassion and practicing it yourself—both hold enormous potential for enlivening your therapy practice and making you a more effective clinician.

We know that compassion is one of the most important factors for creating positive change in psychotherapy (Wampold, 2013). We know this from our own experience as clinicians, as well as over 70 years of outcome research (which I discuss at length in Chapter 2). However, not all of us are aware that compassion is a skill that can be developed through practice. By using the tools and techniques you will learn in this book, you will be able to grow your compassion for your clients and help them find compassion for themselves.

I believe that our highest calling as human beings is to relieve suffering and bring well-being to others and ourselves. I believe compassion makes this possible, and that the development of compassion always begins with *self*-compassion. As the beloved Buddhist teacher Pema Chödrön (2010) says, "In order to have compassion for others, we have to have compassion for ourselves."

As we teach our clients to practice self-compassion, they develop a deep source of calming, soothing, and positive regard within themselves, which makes them more resilient and better able to regulate their emotions. Researchers such as Kristin Neff and Chris Germer have shown that self-compassion training not only decreases depression and anxiety, but also increases happiness and relationship satisfaction (Neff, Kirkpatrick, & Rude, 2007; Neff & Germer, 2013). As clinicians, when we learn how to be more self-compassionate, we naturally begin feeling more compassion for our clients, even the difficult ones.

SELF-COMPASSION AND MINDFULNESS

Self-compassion is intimately related to the practice of mindfulness, both of which have garnered deep respect from some of the most influential voices in the mental health field (Kabat-Zinn, 2003). Mindfulness can be understood as a special way of paying attention. We focus our awareness in the present moment, with complete acceptance of our thoughts, feelings, and bodily sensations. Rather than being lost in regrets about the past or worries about the future, we are completely present in the here and now. Through developing this way of paying attention, we become more grounded, peaceful, resilient, and loving.

In all of the years that I have spent studying with Thich Nhat Hanh, I have learned that it is impossible to truly separate mindfulness and self-compassion. As he would say, you cannot have mindfulness without compassion, and the practice of compassion always begins with compassion toward oneself.

This perspective, which I explore in more depth in Chapters 4 and 5, has the potential to help therapists who are new to mindfulness begin to integrate it into their work, as well as help those who have a strong background in mindfulness gain a deeper understanding of its transformative potential. You don't need to have any background in mindfulness in order to benefit from this book, but if you do, you will find that self-compassion practices have the capacity to add new layers of depth to mindfulness-based therapies such as Dialectical Behavior Therapy (DBT), Acceptance and Commitment Therapy (ACT), Mindfulness-Based Stress Reduction (MBSR), and Mindfulness-Based Cognitive Therapy (MBCT).

THE PROBLEM OF SELF-CRITICISM

Although self-compassion sounds like a pretty simple idea, it isn't easy for most of us. Instead, we have a tendency to judge and criticize ourselves for any way that we fail to measure up to our idealized standards. Even those of us who really value self-compassion can be downright mean to ourselves sometimes. For example, a therapist who was attending one of my trainings said, "I keep trying to teach this one particular client to be more compassionate toward himself, but I'm getting nowhere." He looked really sad and frustrated, so I asked him to picture that client and tell me what thoughts came up for him. He paused for a moment and said, "I'm not helping this man at all. I must be a terrible therapist." I think we can all relate to having thoughts like this from time to time.

However, just because self-criticism is really common doesn't mean that it's harmless. This kind of negative and judgmental thinking is actually at the root of many of our clients' symptoms. It can lead to depression, anxiety, addiction, and even suicide. In fact, researchers have found that self-criticism is one of the biggest predictors of serious mental health problems (Harter, 1993).

You might be asking yourself, if self-criticism is so pervasive and so potentially devastating, what can we do about it? Luckily, it is possible to learn how to relate to ourselves with kindness and compassion.

SELF-COMPASSION VERSUS SELF-ESTEEM

Before we begin learning how to cultivate self-compassion and teach it to our clients, we first need to understand what it means. Self-compassion is actually very different from the concept of self-esteem. Whereas self-esteem is about evaluating oneself positively, self-compassion is about *relating* to oneself with a kind and forgiving attitude (Neff & Vonk, 2009).

Since the 1970s, self-esteem has been one of the most popular concepts in psychology, and for much of that time, it has been regarded as one of the best measures of overall mental health and wellness (Harter, 1993). For decades, researchers believed that self-esteem correlated with success in school, work, and relationships, as well as with most measures of happiness (Kernis, 1993). However, beginning in the mid-1990s, new data have emerged that give us a different picture. Although having low self-esteem and believing that you are a bad person is certainly bad for your mental health, high self-esteem can create real problems as well (Baumeister, Smart, & Boden, 1996).

For so many of us, and especially for our clients, having high self-esteem is tied to comparing ourselves with others. In order to feel good about ourselves, we must believe we are entirely unique, good at everything we do, and *especially that we are better than other people*. How many of us would feel happy if told that our job performance is average? What if your spouse said you were an average partner, or your child looked into your eyes and said, "Mommy, you are an average mommy"? For many of us, being told that we are average feels like being told we are worthless.

This brings up one of the core problems with focusing on self-esteem: It's just not possible for everyone to be above average. It is also impossible for a single person to be above average in every way. In the past decade or so, researchers have found that many people try to protect their self-esteem by putting others down or adopting grossly inaccurate ideas about themselves (Baumeister, Campbell, Krueger, & Vohs, 2003). In fact, someone who really prioritizes having a positive evaluation of him- or herself can become rigidly defensive and competitive. It can lead to a tendency to blame or criticize others and to fragility around receiving negative feedback. This "superiority complex" can come from being too focused on self-esteem, and it is actually an obstacle to developing self-compassion (or compassion for anyone).

What makes self-esteem different from self-compassion is that self-esteem is about a value judgment: We judge ourselves as good or bad, better or worse. On the other hand, when we focus on self-compassion, it doesn't really matter how we compare to other people. What matters is kindness and seeing ourselves clearly (Neff & Vonk, 2009). My teacher, Thich Nhat Hanh, talks about these issues in a unique and thought-provoking way. He warns people against the dangers of a superiority complex, an inferiority complex, or an equality complex. In other words, it's not important whether you are better, worse, *or just as good as* other people. What matters is being kind to yourself and others.

COMPASSION FOR OTHERS

If self-compassion is not about praise or positive evaluations, what is it exactly? Let's start by looking at what we mean by *compassion*. If we can understand what compassion for another person looks like, that will help us to know what it means to have compassion for ourselves. I'll tell a brief story about a client that I think illustrates several important elements of compassion.

Jeff, an engineer at a large firm, came to see me because a conflict he was having at work was getting in the way of his job performance and he decided he needed some help. In our first session, he described his colleague, Donald, as the most annoying person he had ever met. He and Donald had been assigned to work together on a major project (despite Jeff's protests), and the project was in danger of failing completely. Donald would almost always miss his deadlines and turn in low-quality work. What made this behavior particularly infuriating for Jeff is that whenever he would confront Donald about his work, Donald would just look down and shrug his shoulders—no apology, and not even an excuse.

Jeff told me: "He thinks I should have to do all of his work for him while he takes home a big fat paycheck every week. He doesn't seem to care about anything so long as he's still making his money. I wish they would just fire him." Jeff had become so resentful about doing all of the work on the project that he developed a major procrastination problem. He just couldn't force himself to work on the project because it felt so unfair.

In our first session, I mostly just listened. At the end of our time, I asked him to go and learn everything he could about Donald's home life before our next session. From Jeff's descriptions, I guessed there was going to be something there.

When Jeff came back a week later, he said he had been blown away by what he learned. It turned out that Donald was in the middle of a messy divorce. He hadn't seen his children in weeks, and was living in a motel while he looked for an apartment. Donald was depressed and not handling it well. He hadn't reached out for any help and was not very good at self-care. As soon as he heard everything Donald was going through, Jeff apologized for getting so mad at him. Donald said how much it meant to him that Jeff had asked about his life and listened to him, and he then apologized for the poor quality of his work. Jeff encouraged Donald to explain the situation to their boss and ask for more help on the project, which was immediately granted. He also encouraged Donald to find a therapist.

After Jeff finished explaining everything that had happened over the week, I asked about the issues that had brought him into therapy. Was he more productive at work and less bothered by Donald? Jeff said, "Well, the productivity thing is way better, especially because we now have a third full-time person on the project. About Donald, I used to hate him but now I just feel bad for him. If everything that is happening to him were happening to me, I would be floored. I might not make it into work at all. I wish I could help him. I mean, I'm glad he will be getting some help from a therapist, but I wish I could do more."

I asked Jeff to pause right there and give himself a minute to feel all of that. I instructed him to picture Donald and really let himself feel how much he would like to help if he could. I said not to worry about whether there was anything he could really do, but just to feel how much he would like to help if he could. Jeff said, "Yeah, wow. It makes me a little sad, but it actually feels good. I think I'm going to talk with him again and see if there is anything more I could do."

I believe that Jeff's experience is a concrete example of compassion, which the Dalai Lama (1995) defines as "a sensitivity to the suffering of self and others, with a deep commitment to try to relieve it" (p. 16). It also helps illustrate a point that Thich Nhat Hanh often makes when teaching about compassion: When we understand someone deeply enough, compassion arises naturally. All Jeff needed was to learn about the suffering Donald was going through, and a huge change happened in his attitude. He went from active hostility to a deep desire to help.

THE THREE KEY INGREDIENTS OF COMPASSION

Thich Nhat Hanh often says that understanding leads to compassion, but what exactly does he mean? He certainly doesn't mean that any kind of understanding leads to compassion. If I understand that someone had eggs for breakfast or was born in Indiana, that isn't necessarily going to help me feel any differently about them. I believe there are three specific types of understanding—the three key ingredients—that have the power to create compassion within us.[1] We will first consider these key ingredients in terms of compassion for another person, and then we will see how they apply in an example of self-compassion.

1. *We understand that the person suffers.* Jeff's attitude changed as soon as he saw how much Donald was suffering. At first, Jeff assumed that Donald was acting out of pure selfishness, but when he realized what a hard time Donald was having, he could see the situation more clearly, and compassion was the natural result. When we don't see the role that suffering plays in how people are acting, we come up with all kinds of mistaken views about why they are doing what they're doing. We might think they are selfish, cruel, or enjoy making us miserable. If that's how we think about someone, we aren't going to feel much compassion. Instead, we feel angry and frustrated, like Jeff did, or we might feel sad and powerless. When we feel that way about someone, it can be helpful to reflect on how that person might be suffering.

2. *We understand the person wants to be happy and is attempting (however unskillfully) to create happiness for themselves and others.* When Jeff first learned about what Donald was going through, imagine if he had thought: "This guy just wants to suffer. He isn't doing anything to help himself, and I'm not going to waste my time on a lost cause." That kind of thinking would have led to a really different result. Instead, when Jeff learned about Donald's suffering, he also recognized

that Donald wanted to be happy and needed help. We all do things that cause problems for ourselves and others, or we might not know how to help ourselves out of a difficult situation, but that doesn't necessarily mean we like to suffer.

It's possible to have every intention to create happiness for ourselves and other people, and just not know how. For example, if my son stole something, I might lose my temper and yell at him. I'm not yelling because I enjoy making him suffer. I'm yelling because I don't want him to make choices that will cause more suffering in his life. I want him to be happy, and I can't think of a better way to make that happen in that moment than to yell at him. If someone could tell me what to do so that he would feel really loved and never steal anything again, I'd certainly prefer to do that.

In fact, I'd like you to stop and think about one of the worst things you've ever done in your life—a choice that you deeply regret. Once you've chosen something, reflect on this: If, in that moment, you had known how you could have created happiness (or safety or whatever basic need) for yourself and still made others happy, would you have chosen to do that? Really take a minute to consider this question. If, in that difficult moment, you could have come up with some way to take care of your own needs and make other people happy, would you have rather done that?

I've asked this question to many clients and the answer is almost always the same. Even the actions we regret most weren't done from a truly malicious intent. Plenty of people will say that they did want to cause pain to another person, because it was the only way they could think of to take care of their own needs. If they could have made themselves feel safe or understood, etc., without harming the other person, they would have preferred that, but they didn't know how. When we see this basic motivation toward happiness in ourselves and others, compassion becomes more possible.

3. *We understand that we are not fundamentally separate from each other.* If you are a person who suffers and wants to be happy, then you have a lot in common with every other person on

the planet. This is something that we all share and that connects us. It is part of what it means to be human. Seeing that we are all in this situation together—that we all struggle, want to be happy, and don't always know how to make that happen—this is the third key ingredient to compassion.

When Jeff told me what Donald was going through, one of the first things he said was how he might feel if he were facing the same problems. He put himself in Donald's "shoes" and could identify with how his coworker was feeling. He saw that they were not fundamentally separate, but that they were both human beings who want to be happy and don't want to suffer. There is a genuine feeling of connection that comes from this insight.

Another part of this understanding is seeing that the other person's happiness is connected to our own. Jeff realized that helping Donald was also helping himself. If he could do something to make Donald feel just a little happier, that would make him happy too. When we recognize how connected we are, compassion comes more easily.

The Dalai Lama (2006) beautifully describes these three ingredients in his statement: "Human beings by nature want happiness and do not want suffering. With that feeling everyone tries to achieve happiness and tries to get rid of suffering. . . . Basically, from the viewpoint of real human value we are all the same" (p.180). When we can see that other people are just like we are—that they suffer and want to be happy—what emerges is a special kind of alliance. We want them to have relief from their suffering and to be happy, just like they do. It's a deep kind of wishing them well. It's a *wanting* for them not to suffer and to be happy. This desire often leads to action that is about trying to help the situation. However, if you realize there is nothing more you can do, there is still a tremendous amount of power in just wishing someone well in a focused and conscious way.

COMPASSION FOR ONESELF

So what does it look like to have this kind of compassion for oneself? Let's look at another example to see how these three key ingredients apply to self-compassion.

Janet, a professor of economics, came to see me about some anxiety she was experiencing during teaching. She was the kind of person who was great at math and research, but not as good at interacting with people. She was an intense perfectionist and very driven. Her success in academia had been the result of her excellent research, but she had always had difficulty teaching and working collaboratively.

The problem she described as her reason for coming into therapy was that she had begun to dread giving lectures. Just thinking about an upcoming lecture would make her feel queasy. I asked if she knew what about teaching made her feel so uncomfortable, and she said, "I'm just not good enough at it. I know the concepts, but sometimes I can't articulate them well enough and I see the students look confused and I know it's my fault. I hate it."

We talked more about Janet's experience of teaching and got a really clear sense of the role that self-criticism was playing in her problem. Any time Janet didn't articulate a concept as well as she would have liked, she would get extremely frustrated with herself and start thinking, "I'm such an idiot! Why am I even allowed to teach? They should fire me because I don't belong here." It was easy to see why giving herself no margin of error as a teacher, which wasn't a natural area of strength for her, was creating a lot of problems.

Over the next few weeks, I learned that this powerful self-criticism had been an important motivating tool for Janet since at least junior high school. She believed that her relentless work ethic and the success that had come from it were the direct result of holding herself to very high standards. At the same time, she could see how this tool had actually begun to interfere with her ability to achieve. She referred to her inner critic as her "slave driver" and said, "I used to beat myself up and it would get me to work harder. Now, you've helped me see how, in this case, I'm so scared of the slave driver that I'm freezing up." Although this new insight was valuable, Janet expressed being scared that if she lost her slave driver, she wouldn't be able to motivate herself enough to succeed at such a demanding job.

I suggested that we try an exercise in which she would imagine giving a lecture and see what it would be like for her to practice self-compassion in a moment like that. I asked Janet to recall a recent lecture in which she felt that she wasn't living up to her expectations and to picture herself back there. When she really felt like she was there, I asked what thoughts were coming up, and she reported a lot of the same self-criticism: "I'm not saying this right. What's wrong with me?"

I asked Janet to try saying to herself, "I really want to do a good job, and I'm having a hard time. This isn't easy for me." I explained that she isn't making an excuse, but just stating a fact. She was quiet for about a minute and then said, "Yeah. That's really what's going on. I'm trying and it's not easy for me. It felt a little scary at first, when you first had me say it, but then I felt a big relief. I'm not making an excuse. It's just true. Just naming it like that makes me feel a little better." At this point, I had helped her to name what was going on without judging it. This very initial experience of mindfulness is an important step toward self-compassion.

I told Janet that I was glad she was feeling better, and asked if she wanted to continue with the exercise. She did, and I asked her to picture herself back in that same scene, giving a lecture and not feeling as eloquent as she would like. When she felt like she was there, I asked her to try saying, "I'm trying to do something, and I really want to do it well. It's hard for me, and whatever feelings come up for me are OK. It's OK for me to really want something and not to be able to do it." Her eyes were closed and she was quiet for a while before she said, "That felt really powerful. Just giving myself the permission to want something and not to be able to do it. It's a huge relief. I think this is going to help me." This was another important step toward self-compassion. Janet had a deeper experience of mindfulness in which she was able to accept her feelings in a difficult moment.

Janet and I spent a few more weeks practicing this kind of attitude until she was ready to take it a step further. At that point, I asked her to picture herself at a time when she felt insecure giving a lecture. When she felt like she was really there, I asked what thoughts were coming up now, and was glad to learn that she wasn't having the same kind of harsh self-criticism that she had reported a few weeks earlier. She said, "I know I'm struggling here, but it's OK. People struggle and it's hard." She looked at me and commented, "I still feel insecure, but it's much better than it used to be." Now, I asked her to try saying to herself, "I know you are struggling and I am here for you. I want to support you any way I can." She looked a little confused. "Do you want me to say that to myself? Like I'm talking to myself?" I told her to try those words and see how they feel.[2]

Janet closed her eyes and said out loud, "Janet, I know you are struggling and I am here for you. I want to support you any way I can." She was quiet for a moment and then said it again, this time adding, "You are doing your best, and I see that." She started crying softly, and after another minute or two of silence said, "That feels really good. I don't think I've ever been so nice to myself. It makes me cry. And it makes me really feel like I'm OK being who I am. Thank you so much for this."

Although it took Janet a while to internalize this attitude and develop it into a habit, her relationship to teaching began to improve right away. Looking at her experience, you can see the three key ingredients at work: (1) She recognized herself as someone who was suffering and (2) that she was doing her best. (3) She could also see that she was not alone in her struggles—that everyone struggles sometimes. Finally, she was able to *wish herself well* in a way that felt deep and transformative. In this session, I knew that Janet had succeeded at getting in touch with self-compassion because that experience of wishing herself well had created a powerfully positive emotional response. In Chapters 6–10 you will learn how to custom-tailor exercises like these for almost any client. Figure 1.1 provides a succinct overview of the three key ingredients.

FIGURE 1.1. The Three Key Ingredients of Self-Compassion

"I know I'm suffering."

+

"I know I'm trying to create happiness."

+

"I'm not alone in this."

"I'm wishing myself well."

THE NEAR ENEMIES OF SELF-COMPASSION

Initially, Janet was afraid that if she stopped criticizing herself, she would lose her motivation to achieve. However, as she developed more compassion toward herself, especially toward her insecurities, she found that she was able to be more productive than ever. She said, "It's like instead of being my own slave driver, I've become my own cheerleader, and it feels a lot healthier." Although her fears were ultimately unfounded, these kinds of concerns are very common.

In the Buddhist tradition, there is a concept of *near enemies* that I find really helpful for understanding the practice of self-compassion. A near enemy is a quality that is similar enough that you can mistake it for the real thing, but it's actually a type of opposite. For example, one near enemy of self-compassion would be self-indulgence. At first, Janet believed that if she stopped being so hard on herself, it would mean giving herself complete permission to put forth no effort at all. In other words, she thought that self-compassion meant becoming completely self-indulgent. She learned that the reality is actually very different and that it is possible to encourage herself with kindness. In fact, researchers Breines and Chen (2012) found that self-compassion is actually associated with a greater motivation to improve.

If you are wondering whether there are any situations in which self-compassion is not helpful or could even be harmful, I believe the answer is no. These kinds of fears generally come from mistaking self-compassion for one of its near enemies, so let's take a moment and examine a few of them:

- *Self-indulgence*: Janet could have believed, "Being kind to myself means not trying to push myself to do anything. I can do whatever I want, or nothing at all, and kindness means just accepting that and celebrating it." This is actually not compassion because it's based on ignoring the part of herself that really *wants* to succeed and contribute to the lives of others.
- *Self-pity*: Janet could have believed, "I'm in pain and I need to stop trying to pretend I'm not. My suffering is important and I need to let myself cry." This statement can be completely healthy in a certain context, but if she never connects with the kind of *wishing herself well* that actually brings some relief to her suffering, then she is missing the most important part of self-compassion.
- *Passivity*: Compassion naturally leads to action. If we see that our baby is hungry, we don't just empathize with her hunger. We feed her. Although self-compassion can be a powerful force with no explicit action accompanying it, it's also important to remember that real compassion sometimes dictates that we make a concrete change to some aspect of our lives.
- *Egotism*: Viewing oneself as better than another person or being overly involved with one's own needs at the expense of another's is not practicing self-compassion. This kind of egotism comes from conflating self-compassion with self-esteem. As mentioned earlier, self-compassion is not concerned with comparing oneself to others; it values everyone's happiness.

SELF-COMPASSION IN PSYCHOTHERAPY

Let's take a moment and reflect on the question, "What is it that heals suffering?" There is a saying that "Time heals all wounds," but for those of us who work in mental health, we know that's not always true. People can hang onto their suffering for a very long time. So if time alone is not enough, what is it that heals suffering? In Buddhist psychology, it is said that compassion is the energy that heals suffering (Hanh, 2011). Compassion is applied to suffering like salve to a wound, and when this happens, the result is healing and transformation. It doesn't matter if the source of that compassion is oneself or another person. What matters is that somehow *compassion makes direct contact with our pain*.

> *It doesn't matter if the source of that compassion is oneself or another person. What matters is that somehow compassion makes direct contact with our pain.*

Buddhist psychology views compassion in a way that is similar to how Carl Rogers viewed it. Through his research, Rogers (1957) found that one of the most important factors for effective therapy is compassion, and modern psychotherapy outcome research has confirmed this finding (see Chapter 2 for details). The more our clients feel understood and that we truly care about them, the more likely they are to get better (Flückiger, Del Re, Wampold, Symonds, & Horvath, 2012). Therefore, the practice of self-compassion supports effective therapy in two vital ways: (1) We can help our clients become a source of compassion for themselves; and (2) we can use these practices to be happier and generate more compassion for our clients.

For most of the history of psychotherapy, the therapist has been seen as the main source of compassion in the relationship. However, the explosion of interest in mindfulness and self-compassion has expanded our understanding of how compassion can be utilized for emotional change. We now know that clients can develop the ability to be their own source of healing compassion through explicit training. This will be the core focus of the rest of this book. We will explore various clinical contexts and learn how to guide clients into a direct experience of self-compassion. Once they have their first successful experience, we will then focus on helping them strengthen this capacity through deliberate practice.

It's not always easy to feel compassion for our clients. We all have had the experience of being triggered or annoyed by a client from time to time, and self-compassion practices can be helpful here too. One of my first clients, when I was in my practicum, was a young woman who said that she was dating a really nice guy who was kind and funny and supportive. She told me she was cheating on him with an artist who was addicted to crack and kept stealing money from her. My first reaction was to think, "What?!? What's wrong with you? That's a horrible choice. You should just stop!"

Luckily, I had already been a serious student of Buddhism for many years at that point, and I recognized that I was not feeling compassion for her. I bit my tongue and got through the rest of that session the best I could. Then when I got home, I brought up the image of this client in my own meditation practice. I pictured her and felt all of the tension and aversion that came up in my body. I spent some time just letting myself feel those feelings and began to send myself some compassion. As my mind settled down, I quickly recognized that she reminded me of some people from my own life who had made bad choices and created a lot of suffering. I let myself think of those times in my past and directed compassion at those painful memories. After about 90 minutes of practicing like this, I felt much calmer and more peaceful. Now, when I pictured my client again, my heart went out to her. I could see how confused and ashamed of herself she was, and how deeply she wanted help. My whole way of seeing her changed because I was able to send *myself* compassion when I needed it.

Beginning on that day in the Buddhist monastery outside of San Diego, I have experienced how self-compassion can transform suffering over and over again. My deep intention is for this book to serve as a guide to applying this powerful practice in almost any clinical situation.

Chapter 2

THE SCIENCE OF
SELF-COMPASSION

In this chapter I contend that any therapist whose work is truly informed by all of the relevant science would view cultivating self-compassion as one of the most important elements of therapy. We will explore five distinct areas of research—neuroscience, cognitive science, psychotherapy outcome research, self-compassion research, and positive psychology—in order to make this case. It's my hope that by the end of the chapter, you will view self-compassion as a vital part of effective therapy and something supported by cutting-edge science.

NEUROSCIENCE: SELF-COMPASSION AND THE BRAIN

What effect does practicing self-compassion have on your brain? The short answer is that it strengthens the parts of your brain that make you happier, more resilient, and more attuned to others. It can also comfort negative emotions in the present and even permanently heal painful memories from the past or change negative core beliefs.

To get a more detailed understanding of this science, we will explore the work of three of the most respected affective neuroscientists in the world: Richard Davidson, Jaak Panksepp, and Joseph LeDoux.

Davidson and the Dalai Lama

In researching for this chapter, I spoke with Richard Davidson, the highly respected neuroscientist from the University of Wisconsin–Madison. As a recipient of the American Psychological Association's Distinguished Scientific Contribution Award and regular participant in the Mind and Life Dialogues with the Dalai Lama, Davidson is a legend in the field and one of the foremost experts in the world on the science of emotion. After discussing his research, I asked Professor Davidson what he would want all therapists to know about his work. He said, "Well-being can be learned, but it requires practice. There is no substitute for practice."

Davidson has been studying the emotional systems of the brain since the 1980s. His early research was about mapping the brain's emotional centers (using functional magnetic resonance imaging [fMRI]), as well as learning what kinds of brain waves (using an electroencephalograph [EEG]) are associated with different emotions. In a study, he might put subjects in an fMRI tube and map their brain activity. Then he would make them happy, sad, or scared (e.g., by showing them an emotional video), and map their brain activity again. After decades of methodical research, Davidson had become one of the world's leading experts on the differences between a happy brain and an unhappy one.

Davidson began researching the effects of self-compassion when he was invited by the Dalai Lama to study the brains of long-term meditators. Davidson had had a private interest in meditation since he was a young man and embraced the opportunity.

His first study (Davidson, 2012) asked a small group of Tibetan monks, each of whom had over 10,000 hours of intensive meditation training, to practice different styles of meditation while he measured the effects on their brains. He found that when they were engaged in compassion meditation—sending compassion to themselves and all beings (a practice we'll learn in Chapter 6)—they showed the highest readings ever recorded in the happiness centers of their brains. For those of you who are interested in neuroanatomy, in all these monks, the left prefrontal cortex was much more highly active than the right, they showed an extremely high level of connectivity between their left prefrontal cortex and amygdala, and their brains were producing gamma waves with unprecedented levels of amplitude and synchrony. In plain English, they had the happiest brains that science had ever documented.

However, Davidson couldn't say for sure that this extraordinary happiness was the result of their meditation training. He knew it was possible, although unlikely, that the monks were just born this way. He needed to do some more research.

Davidson's next study (2012) brought in people who had never practiced meditation before. He put them in fMRI tubes to observe their brain activity and taught them the same compassion practice the monks had used. He observed that the practice had a strong effect on the happiness centers of their brains, but not nearly as strong as it did for the monks, who had been training in this practice for decades. This study helped Davidson establish that compassion meditation can create happiness in anyone, and that more training seems to improve the effect.

Finally, Davidson (2012) took this study one step further. Using another group of people who were completely new to meditation, he measured how their brains responded to compassion practice (just like in the last study). Then he had them take an 8-week intensive meditation course. When he measured their brains at the end of the course, he confirmed his theory. This intensive training had resulted in the subjects having a much stronger happiness response when they meditated, as well as a significantly greater level of happiness *while resting*. The training had not only improved their ability to create happiness using compassion meditation, they had also developed a happier temperament. This study was an empirical demonstration of Davidson's core message: Well-being can be learned, but it requires practice.

Based on this research, it is safe to say that as our clients develop the ability to send themselves compassion, the happiness centers in their brains are strengthened. It is also true that no other intervention has been shown to have a stronger effect on developing happiness than self-compassion.[1]

Panksepp and the Basic Emotional Circuits

While Davidson has spent his career mapping human brains, Jaak Panksepp, the Estonian-born scientist and originator of the term *affective neuroscience,* has focused on understanding the basic emotional circuitry that is shared by every mammal, from humans to rats. His research has identified the existence of seven primary emotional circuits in the brain.[2] These seven well-defined neural pathways produce the following basic emotions (Panksepp, 1998):

- Care Circuit: This positive circuit extends from the hypothalamus to the ventral tegmental area (VTA) and into the Seeking Circuit (point 6). It generates oxytocin and endogenous opioids that have been shown to soothe negative emotions. It creates the kind of positive affect that is calm and contented, and it is activated by the practice of self-compassion.
- Play Circuit: This positive circuit is associated with the experiences of joy and spontaneity. It also reduces negative affect and, according to Panksepp, the mental health field would benefit by making greater use of it. When we encourage clients to engage in enjoyable activities or use humor in therapy, we are recruiting the power of this system.
- Fear Circuit: This negative circuit helps us avoid danger by mobilizing the fight–flight–freeze response.
- Grief Circuit: This negative circuit activates in response to loss or separation and induces sadness or panic. Panksepp believes it is designed to solicit care from others.

- Rage Circuit: This negative circuit activates in response to a threat. Like the other two negative circuits, it is experienced as a form of stress.

- Seeking Circuit: This circuit is largely dopamine-mediated and creates enthusiasm, interest, and motivation. Panksepp considers it neutral because it can enhance positive or negative emotions.
- Lust Circuit: This is the circuit that regulates sexual arousal. Panksepp also considers it neutral.

These seven primary affective circuits work like primary colors in the sense that they can be mixed in different ways to create the full richness of human emotion. Panksepp's work is vast, and I strongly recommend all interested clinicians read his latest book, *The Archaeology of Mind* (Panksepp & Biven, 2012).

The key point here is that the practice of self-compassion recruits the Care Circuit to produce oxytocin and endogenous opioids.[3] These bonding chemicals act to comfort our negative emotions and reduce distress. From your brain's perspective, comforting yourself is almost identical to being nurtured by someone else. In Chapter 6, we will explore various practices for activating the Care Circuit and getting these "feel-good" chemicals flowing. Chapters 7 and 8 will cover practices that can recruit this circuit to heal suffering.

LeDoux and Transforming the Past in the Present

Joseph LeDoux heads a neuroscience lab at New York University where he studies memory. Thanks to him and his colleagues, we know that our memories are not etched in stone. When a memory is retrieved, it enters a state of being changeable (neuroscientists call it *labile*). During that time, it makes new associations with whatever is happening in the present. This realization has huge implications for therapy (Schiller et al., 2009; Monfils, Cowansage, Klann & LeDoux, 2009).

Here's what it looks like in an experiment (Hupbach, Gomez, Hardt, & Nadel, 2007). Look at the following list of items and try to remember them. Close your eyes and see if you can recall them. If you can, they have been safely placed in your *short-term* memory. Now imagine that you're taking part in a study and you've been asked to remember these items for 3 days.

List One
1. Spoon
2. Rock
3. Bottle
4. Dinosaur

Tomorrow morning, you wake up and drive to the researchers' office, where they give you a second list of items to memorize. If you are in Group A, the researchers give you only the new list. If you are in Group B, the researchers ask you to recall the items in List One and recite them before they give you List Two. Here is your second list.

List Two
1. Dog
2. Crowbar
3. Magazine
4. Knitting needles

On the third day, you return to the researchers' office and they ask you to write down each list. If you were in Group A, you would have an easy time remembering both of them. However, if you were in Group B, you would likely confuse which objects belong to which list. You would put objects from List One into List Two, and vice versa. This mistake is caused by a neural process called *memory reconsolidation*—which is the same process we will use to heal past suffering and change negative core beliefs.

This is how it happened: When you learned List One, it was briefly placed into your short-term memory and then *consolidated* into your long-term memory. You can imagine it was stored in the form of a new neural network in your brain.[4] If you were in Group B, you were asked to recall List One right before learning List

Two. As I mentioned earlier, when a memory is activated, it becomes changeable and makes new associations with whatever is happening in the present. When you recited List One, that memory became activated. As you learned List Two, new associations were formed and the old memory actually changed. When List One was put back into your long-term memory–or *reconsolidated*— it was in a new form because it was now associated with the objects from List Two. This is why you would get confused about which objects belonged to which list. Group A participants didn't have this problem because they learned the second list without having the memory of the first list activated.

We now understand that all memories are reconsolidated every time they are recalled (Nader, Schafe & LeDoux, 2000). It might seem strange, but think about the wisdom of this process. Evolution favors traits that foster survival. The ability to update old views with new information helps us to make better choices. On the other hand, there is not a lot of evolutionary value in our long-term memories being super-accurate. Long ago, the ability to learn from new information was "recognized," in an evolutionary sense, as more important than storing accurate memories about the past.

In order to fully appreciate the implications of memory reconsolidation in therapy, we need to be clear about what neuroscientists mean by a "memory." Most of us use the word *memory* to mean an experience from the past that we can consciously recall. We also say that we *remember* facts. However, neuroscientists use the word *memory* much more broadly.

Absolutely everything you know—from how to speak English, to how to brush your teeth, to core beliefs about your value as a person—is stored in the patterns of connections in the neural networks of your brain. A neuroscientist would use the word *memory* to refer to all of that. In other words, anything stored in your brain is a memory. There are dozens of types of memories. The types we most often associate with the word *memory* are episodic (e.g., I remember when I had breakfast with my grandmother last week) and declarative (e.g., I remember the fact that New Delhi is the capital of India).

However, most of our core beliefs and schemas, as well as most emotional memories in general, are called *implicit memories* by neuroscientists (Tobias, Kihlstrom, & Schacter, 1992) because they affect us without our explicit awareness.

This is why neuroscientists believe the main cause of psychological symptoms is not "imbalanced chemicals" (Lacasse & Leo, 2005), but rather implicit memories in the emotional centers of the brain. As therapists, one of our main jobs is helping our clients transform these symptom-generating implicit memories through the process of reconsolidation.

As therapists, one of our main jobs is helping our clients transform these symptom-generating implicit memories through the process of reconsolidation.

That might sound pretty complicated, but it's actually not. As I mentioned earlier, all that is required for a memory to be reconsolidated is for it to be recalled. There is a lot of evidence that the more vividly it is remembered, the more changeable it becomes (Deębiec, Doyère, Nader, & LeDoux, 2006). Then, while the memory is being activated (whether it's a memory of abuse or a core belief about oneself), it can be associated with new information. Bringing up old memories can be tricky—which is why Chapter 9 focuses on special situations such as working with people who have experienced trauma, addiction, or psychosis.

Panksepp believes that if distressing memories are reconsolidated while the Care Circuit is active, they become less distressing. In other words, if a client is receiving compassionate attention from a therapist or is practicing self-compassion while connecting with painful memories or negative core beliefs, that juxtaposition is a recipe for healing *at a molecular level*. In my view, this process is the most relevant application of neuroscience to the mental health field.

COGNITIVE SCIENCE:
THE POWER OF PRACTICE

Cognitive science is different from neuroscience. In fact, cognitive scientists generally don't study the brain. They are psychologists, philosophers, and even computer scientists who are interested in developing models of how people think. They are particularly interested in common logical errors, because they want to create models that really think like people. In this section I review three famous experiments by cognitive scientists and then discuss how they can help us understand more about developing self-compassion.

Dan Kahneman is a Nobel Prize-winning psychologist at Princeton and author of the best-selling book *Thinking, Fast and Slow* (2011). If you like this section, I highly recommend reading that book. When Kahneman was a young professor, he discovered that it is possible to measure mental effort through the dilation of a person's pupils (Kahneman & Beatty, 1966). Let's play a game to illustrate his point. The game is called *plus one*. I will give you three numbers. Read the three numbers, add one to each of them, and then say them back.

Here are the numbers: 3, 4, and 6. Add 1 to each of them, and say the answer out loud. If you said 4, 5, and 7, then you understood the directions. That is *plus one*.

Now, imagine there had been a camera focused on your eyes and the image was projected up on a big screen. Before playing, your pupils would have been a certain size. Then when you looked at those numbers and started adding, they would have gotten bigger until you came up with the answer. Once you had the answer, they would have returned to normal. Kahneman discovered this fact and was really excited about it. Experimenting further, he realized that people's eyes dilate more if the game is harder. If we were to play *plus three* (I give you some numbers and you add 3 to each of them), your pupils would dilate much more than they did playing *plus one*.

One day, Dan Kahneman was playing *plus three* with a friend who was a math professor. Imagine the math professor sitting in a chair with a camera focused on his eyes and Kahneman over by a screen measuring his pupils with a ruler. When they were finished, Kahneman started asking his friend about what he had done over the weekend. The math professor said he had seen some friends, maybe gone to a barbecue or something like that. For whatever reason, Kahneman hadn't turned off the camera and he was completely surprised by what he saw. While his friend was talking about his weekend, his pupils didn't dilate at all.

Kahneman was really interested in computer modeling. He would have people do different tasks, see how much their pupils would dilate, and then compare his findings to how complicated those tasks would be for a computer. Up until then, he had shown that the more complicated the process would be for a computer, the more that people's pupils would dilate. However, now he was confused.

If you have ever tried to interact with Siri or any other computer program that tries to have a conversation with you, you know that our computers today aren't powerful enough to have a natural conversation. The computer I'm using to write this book could play *plus one, plus three,* or *plus whatever-you-want* without any difficulty, but it isn't powerful enough to have a natural conversation.

This is exactly what confused Kahneman. If our pupils dilate with a simple process, and then dilate more with a more complicated one, why would they not dilate at all when executing a process as complex as having a conversation? Take a moment and guess why you think that might be. We'll return to this question soon.

Another famous experiment in cognitive science is based on this word problem:

A bat and a ball together cost $1.10. The bat costs $1.00 more than the ball does. How much is the ball?

There's a really good chance that you came up with the answer, 10¢. That is by far the most common answer people give to this problem, although it's actually wrong. Take a moment to look at the problem again. If the ball were 10¢, and the bat costs $1.00 more than the ball does, then the bat would be $1.10. That would make the total $1.20. The right answer is 5¢. That makes the bat $1.05, and the total is $1.10.

Many of us go into the mental health field because we are not particularly interested in math, so that's *not* why this problem is interesting. It's interesting because when you give this problem to PhD candidates in math and statistics at Harvard, MIT, and Princeton, more than 50% of them will also say 10¢. Why is that? These are people who love math and are really good at it, yet they also get this question wrong. Take a moment to guess why that might be. We'll return to this issue as well.

Let's consider one more famous experiment from cognitive science. However, by this point you might assume it's a trick question, so don't worry about answering it.

> *An individual has been described by a neighbor as follows: "Steve is very shy and withdrawn, invariably helpful but with very little interest in people or in the world of reality. A meek and tidy soul, he has a need for order and structure, and a passion for detail." Is Steve more likely to be a librarian or a farmer?*

If you give this question to a large sample of people, most of them will say he's more likely a librarian. However, what is interesting about this question is what occurs to almost no one. When people hear this question, they never think about how many male librarians there are in this country compared to how many male farmers. In fact, there are about 60 male farmers in the United States for every male librarian. This is a question that is about probability (i.e., what is more likely), but instead of thinking about the numbers, most of us think about the stereotype.

The Two-System Model of Cognition

Putting these experiments together with many others, cognitive scientists have come up with something they call *dual process theory* or the *two-system model of cognition*. There are two distinct cognitive systems at work in our minds that are named (some-what *un*poetically) System 1 and System 2.

System 1 is comprised of our automatic, effortless thinking processes. These are the thoughts that happen on their own, without any effort from us. System 1 answers questions like what is 2 + 2, and makes us turn suddenly in the direction of a loud bang. It also drives a car for us on an empty highway or reads large words on a billboard. When driving past a billboard with one big word written on it, we practically can't help but read it. That is the work of System 1.

In Kahneman's book *Thinking, Fast and Slow,* System 1 is the fast-thinking system. It happens instantly without any effort, and one of the ways it's able to process information so quickly is that it takes lots of shortcuts. One of System 1's favorite shortcuts is to use stories and stereotypes to make predictions, rather than really thinking about probabilities. The librarian question is an example of our minds choosing stereotypes over probability in order to solve a problem with greater speed and less effort.

Further, when we don't have enough information to come to a conclusion about something (which is a lot of the time), System 1 will fill in the missing details and answer the question anyway. One of my favorite examples of this comes from Michael Gazzaniga's (2012) split-brain research. People who underwent a procedure that severed their corpus callosum (the main connection between the right and left hemispheres of the brain) as a treatment for debilitating seizures participated in a study in which they were asked to sit in a chair. While they were seated, the researcher flashed a sign that said "WALK" in a way that it was perceived only by the right side of their brains. (It's complicated how they were able to ensure that only one side of the brain could perceive the sign, but you can read Gazzaniga's (2012) account for those details.) Once they saw the sign, the patients would stand up and walk across the room, and then the researcher would ask, "Why are you walking across the room?"

The speech center of the brain (known as Broca's area) is located on the left side of the brain, so it had no awareness of having seen a sign. The sign had only been perceived by the right side of the brain and the connection between the two sides had been cut. In every case, the patient would immediately make up a reason why he or she might be walking across the room: for example, "I'm going to get a drink," or "I need to use the bathroom." Whatever the reason, each patient would believe it completely—which is one of the amazing properties of System 1. When we don't have enough information about what is really happening, System 1 will make up whatever information we're missing and then *pretend that it didn't*. We can see this process working in our own lives as well. If your spouse is late getting home from work and you *just know* what they're doing, that is System 1 filling in details you actually don't have and getting you to react as if those details were real.

System 2, on the other hand, is made up of our deliberate, effortful, intentional thinking. It is the "slow thinking" that causes our pupils to dilate. If I ask you to add 2 + 2, System 1 will answer that instantly. If I ask you to multiply 17 × 24, you will have to turn on System 2. System 1 will answer the question, "What does this word say: BLUE? However, if I ask you to count how many times the letter *o* appears in this paragraph, you have to use System 2. Any kind of thinking that requires effort is performed by System 2.

A couple of interesting properties characterize System 2 as well. First, everyone has a limited amount of System 2 energy. Imagine you were trying to parallel park a car in a tight space and I asked you, "What's 17 × 24?" You would probably say, "I'm parking." Then, when you were finished, you might say, "What did you ask me?" You didn't even hear the question because System 2 was working as hard as it could to avoid hitting those other two cars and couldn't process any more information. There is a famous video in which graduate students pass basketballs around and you are instructed to count how many times the players *wearing white* pass the ball. The players are weaving all around each other and it's a very difficult task. In fact, it's so difficult that when a woman wearing a gorilla suit walks right across the screen, most people literally don't see her. The moral of the video is that when System 2 is working at its capacity, a gorilla can walk right by us and we literally won't see it. (You can watch the video at www.theinvisiblegorilla.com.)

Another interesting property of System 2 is that its capacity goes down if we are tired, hungry, distracted, or experiencing any type of stress. One of the most disturbing examples of this fact comes from research on parole boards. Imagine you are an inmate up for parole. If the parole board hears your case first thing in the morning, your chance of receiving parole would be about 5 times greater than if your case came up right before lunch. The percentages improve again after lunch and then drop for the rest of the day. When we are hungry and tired, we just don't have enough System 2 energy to engage with complex problems, so we rely on System 1's knee-jerk reactions, which, for a parole board, means the answer will usually be "No."

Dual process theory has huge implications for psychotherapy. We recognize that whenever we ask clients to use a new skill, they must use some of their limited budget of System 2 energy. If they have real stressors in their lives—if they are hungry or tired, etc.— they won't have enough extra energy to access their new skill.

However, the mindfulness practices you will learn in Chapters 4 and 5 can increase our System 2 capacity in two ways. First, we know that being distracted or stressed decreases our System 2 energy. Mindfulness has the ability to help us improve our concentration and let go of stress, which gives us access to our full budget of System 2 energy. Second, although it has not yet been shown by research, mindfulness practitioners over the past 2,000 years have recognized that what we now call System 2 can be exercised like a muscle. The more we bring System 2's conscious, deliberate presence into our lives, the greater our capacity becomes for this kind of awareness.

We also know that it is possible for System 2 to change the stories and habits of System 1 with effort and practice. The best example of this phenomenon is the process of learning a new language. Imagine being at your very first German class. The teacher shows you a few words and then says something to you in German. When you try to respond, you will need to use a lot of System 2 effort. However, if you practice enough, someday you will develop some fluency in German and be able to have a conversation with no effort at all. What began as a System 2 process eventually becomes the domain of System 1.

On the other hand, imagine if you planned to learn German by attending a 15-minute class that meets once a month and assigns no homework. You could go to that class for the rest of your life and it's unlikely you would ever develop fluency. Because you never put in the effort, speaking German would always remain effortful.

We all know that the most efficient way to learn a language is through immersion. You go somewhere in Germany where people don't speak English, and within a couple months, you have developed some fluency. In other words, speaking German has become an effortless System 1 process. As anyone who has ever actually done this already knows, an immersion experience in another language is exhausting. You have to use every ounce of System 2 energy just to make it through the day. So it is through investing a huge amount of effort into developing a skill that it is possible for that skill to become an effortless habit.

Another helpful analogy is learning self-defense. Imagine you planned to learn self-defense by watching one class, then waiting until someone attacks you and hoping that you remember what the instructor did. That's obviously not how people learn self-defense. Instead, they practice over and over again until the movements become automatic. If they are ever attacked, they don't need to think. System 1 just knows what to do.

In martial arts, there is a saying: "We don't rise to the level of our aspirations. We fall to the level of our training." In other words, System 2 is not available in a crisis. All we have are the things that have become automatic, System 1 processes. Whether the skill is speaking German, using self-defense, or responding to adversity with compassion, we need to train with enough diligence that the skill becomes part of our System 1.

How can mindfulness and self-compassion become effortless System 1 processes? How can they become the way we respond when we're in a crisis? One way is through an immersion experience like a meditation retreat. A retreat can be a lot like a language immersion experience. We are reminded to come back to our mindfulness and compassion over and over again for days, weeks, or even months at a time. I try to spend at least 60 days on retreat each year and have been fortunate enough to attend a few retreats that were several months long. I can't begin to describe how incredibly helpful these retreats have been for making the practices of mindfulness and compassion an integral part of who I am.

Although not all of us have the chance to go on retreats, we can all find ways to integrate mindfulness and self-compassion practices into our daily lives. There is a saying that the Buddha recommended practicing mindfulness when sitting, standing, walking, or lying down—in other words, all the time. We can develop ways of reminding ourselves to come back to the present moment and connect with our compassion throughout the day.

If you were to visit Thich Nhat Hanh at Plum Village, his monastery in southern France, you would notice that every time you hear a bell, absolutely everyone stops what they are doing and takes three breaths. Conversations stop, people in the kitchen stop chopping vegetables, everyone stops. You would also notice there are a lot of bells. There is a bell 10 minutes before every activity, at the beginning of every activity, during and after every activity, and all the clocks are set to chime every 15 minutes. Thich Nhat Hanh says that living in this way is very conducive to maintaining our mindfulness all day long.

However, since not everyone lives in a retreat center like this, we can find other reminders that can function like bells of mindfulness. For some people, washing dishes is a mindfulness practice. For others, stopping at a red light is a chance to breathe and send compassion to themselves and the other drivers. What is important is creating reminders to help us stop and come back to ourselves as often as we can. The more we bring mindfulness and compassion to every moment of our lives, the more these practices become second nature to us.

PSYCHOTHERAPY OUTCOME RESEARCH

Mindfulness and compassion might be wonderful virtues, but are they truly important for effective therapy? In the last chapter, I stated that a compassionate relationship is one of the most important factors for creating positive change in therapy. However, many proponents of the medical model of mental health would disagree with me. They would tend to minimize the importance of the relationship and the therapist's individual qualities in favor of accurate diagnosis and following specific treatment protocols. A therapist might be joyful or depressed, smart or unintelligent, loving or unemotional. They would say that so long as the therapist makes the correct diagnosis and implements the appropriate techniques faithfully, the client should improve.

The debate between the medical model and the humanistic model (also called the "common factors" or "contextual" model) has raged since the early days of our field. Think back to B. F. Skinner and Carl Rogers as classic examples of these two views.

In his book, *The Great Psychotherapy Debate*, Bruce Wampold (2013) attempts to answer this question conclusively by reviewing the entire history of psychotherapy outcome research with tremendous scientific rigor. His first finding is that all forms of *bona fide* therapy are equally effective when they are performed in equal amounts and by people who believe in them. When you compare cognitive therapy to behavioral therapy, experiential therapy, or psychodynamic treatment, the result is always a tie, *so long as the trial is fair.*

Wampold (2013) also informs us that very few trials are actually designed to be fair. A surprisingly large percentage of psychotherapy research consists of comparing apples to oranges in order to make it look like whatever form of therapy the researchers prefer is "better" than another form. Sometimes researchers compare 8 hours of their favorite therapy to 4 hours of another kind. Sometimes they hand-select expert therapists to represent their school and have random or average therapists represent the other school. Sometimes the researchers themselves will perform their type of therapy and then turn around and perform the method that they don't like (which means it won't be the best possible version of it). It's no surprise that when you manipulate a study in any of these ways, you end up with your preferred therapy "winning." Wampold excludes studies with these types of obvious methodological flaws and finds that in a fair trial, one form of therapy is just as good as any other. If you have heard "experts" claim that one type of therapy is better than another, I strongly suggest you look at Wampold's research. It is likely they are referencing unfair trials.

So if the type of therapy isn't the most important thing, then what is? Saying that different types of therapy are equally good *does not mean* that all therapists are the same. In fact, there are huge differences in how effective different therapists are. Barry Duncan and his colleagues cite studies that show the top therapists in the field are able to help about 75% of their clients, whereas the least effective ones help about 25% (Sparks, Duncan, & Miller, 2008).[5] This difference is huge, and it holds up when you control for working with different populations.

Wampold (2013) concludes that the difference between an excellent therapist and a not-so-great one comes down to who they are as a person and how well they are able to connect with clients. Ultimately he sides with Carl Rogers on the Rogers versus Skinner debates about what makes therapy effective. It's not the specifics of the intervention; it is the unconditional positive regard, empathy, understanding, and authenticity of the therapist. In other words, it is the therapist's ability to create a compassionate alliance with the client.

Let's pause for a moment to seriously consider this finding. If we want to improve as a therapist (and enjoy our work more deeply), then the task at hand is learning how to develop our own authentic compassion. But how is that possible? As Richard Davidson (2012) has demonstrated through his research, we can develop this virtue through deliberate training in mindfulness and self-compassion.

SELF-COMPASSION RESEARCH

There is a growing body of research that specifically explores how self-compassion impacts our mental health and how it differs from self-esteem. Kristin Neff of the University of Texas–Austin and Chris Germer of Harvard University are two of the pioneers of this research. They have developed 5-day and 8-week training programs in Mindful Self-Compassion, and have shown that their program improves measures of self-compassion, compassion for others, mindfulness, and life satisfaction—while decreasing depression, anxiety, and stress (Neff & Germer, 2013). Both Neff (2011) and Germer (2009) have written excellent self-help books about self-compassion that can be recommended to clients.

The *Harvard Business Review* published a piece about some wonderful self-compassion research conducted by Juliana Breines and Serena Chen (2012). They divided people into three groups: One group received an intervention that focused on building self-compassion (kindness and forgiveness toward themselves), one group focused on self-esteem (fostering a positive evaluation of themselves), and one received no intervention. Then all three groups were given a few different types of difficulties to experience, such as taking a difficult math test or reflecting on a personal weakness. The group that had been primed to focus on self-compassion reported significantly greater motivation to improve in the face of difficulties than the other two groups. The researchers' conclusion is that not only does self-compassion feel good, but this kind of attitude also helps us overcome challenges and achieve our goals.

I am currently conducting a study that measures the effect of my own online clinical training course ("Foundations of Self-Compassion") on therapists' levels of effectiveness, and I'm highly optimistic about the results. This training focuses on helping therapists develop mastery in applying self-compassion in their own lives, using self-compassion to improve therapeutic alliance building, and mastering specific interventions with clients. Although results have not been published at the time of this writing, you can find more information at www.timdesmond.net

POSITIVE PSYCHOLOGY: WHAT LEADS TO HAPPINESS?

According to positive psychology research, our attitude and relationships are more important than any other factor in determining our level of happiness. Most external circumstances seem to matter very little, such as how much money we have, our career success, etc. Researchers such as Ed Diener (2009) from the University of Illinois have demonstrated that getting a promotion, buying a new car, or even winning the lottery affect our happiness for only a short period of time. After that, we adjust to the change and return to the level of happiness we had before. Fictional characters like Ebenezer Scrooge or Larry David's character on *Curb Your Enthusiasm* are excellent examples of the fact that if you were unhappy before you got rich, you will probably remain so afterward.

It is important to note that increasing your income does create more happiness if you live in poverty. However, that impact weakens quickly and becomes nonexistent as you approach middle-class. When your household income reaches around $75,000 per year, additional income seems to have no impact on how often you feel happy (Kahneman & Deaton, 2010).

The Harvard Grant Study, led by principal investigator George Vaillant (1977), found that our happiness can be predicted fairly well by a just few simple factors. This study followed over 250 Harvard undergraduates from the time they were 19 years old until they were 80, and measured them in various ways. It concluded that the biggest predictors for happiness were the strength of the subjects' relationships (depth of intimacy as well as breadth of social support) and their ability to frame life's challenges in positive ways.

If all of this is true, then why do we spend so much time and energy trying to improve our material circumstances and so little working on our attitudes or investing in our relationships? Harvard psychologist and author of *Stumbling on Happiness* Dan Gilbert (2009) has a great explanation. He points out that our brains have grown by more than 300% over the past 2 million years, and that most of that growth has been associated with our "experience simulator." We know that the prefrontal cortex has many functions, but one of the main things it does is to simulate experience so we can make decisions without actually having to try everything. Gilbert makes the point that Ben & Jerry didn't have to make a batch of liver and bubblegum ice cream to realize it wouldn't taste very good. They just ran it through their brains' experience simulators. In fact, when you just read the words "liver and bubblegum ice cream," your own experience simulator probably ran a very quick simulation and told you that it would be disgusting.

Gilbert (2009) says that although a human's experience simulator is an extremely helpful resource, it also has some real limitations. One of its biggest problems is that it tends to exaggerate the degree to which different situations or external circumstances will affect our happiness. Take a moment and ask your experience simulator which it would prefer for just an hour a day of focused work: You can have $200,000,000—or you could spend an hour a day to have a significantly more positive attitude?

Hearing those options, most people's experience simulator would be screaming, "Take the money!!" However, we just learned that people who win the lottery rarely end up happier than they were before. In fact, many of them become less happy because their friends and family begin constantly asking them for money. On the other hand, having a positive attitude is one of the best predictors of happiness. So why does our experience simulator lead us astray?

According to Gilbert (2009), there are a few reasons. One of the major ones is that our experience simulator doesn't use a huge amount of detail when imagining what a possible situation would be like. When you imagined getting the money, you likely thought about some of the things you could do with that money that you can't do now, or things you wouldn't have to do anymore. However, it's unlikely you thought about how your friends and family would start to treat you differently, or how moving to a fancier home would mean living in a community of people you might not like, or how you still might worry about whether people really like you. This is a tendency Gilbert calls "incomplete imagining," and it is one of the main reasons our experience simulator is so focused on improving our external conditions.

The moral of the story is that it can be really helpful to temper our experience simulator's messages about how to create happiness in our lives with some solid evidence. Despite what this part of your brain tells you, improving your attitude and your relationships will lead to much greater happiness than money or fame. Finally, research by Kristin Neff (Neff et al., 2007) and Mark Leary (Leary, Tate, Adams, Batts Allen, & Hancock, 2007) has shown that self-compassion has the ability to improve our relationships and our attitude in exactly the ways that science (and traditional wisdom) tells us are the true paths to happiness.

CONCLUSION

If you haven't noticed by now, I really love science. I try to be as informed as possible about research with mental health implications. When we examine all of this evidence, I believe it becomes clear that self-compassion (for the client and the therapist) is one of the most important elements of effective therapy.

Chapter 3

BASIC CLINICAL PRINCIPLES

Whenever we learn a new technique, there is always the question of how to integrate it into our work with clients in a way that feels authentic. Many of us have a tendency to try to emulate another person's style when we're learning something new. However, as you move through the rest of this book, I strongly suggest that you reflect on all of the concepts and practices that are presented here in terms of how they relate to your own experience. Experiment with different ideas and try applying them to your own life or to your clients. Use the ideas that make sense to you, and don't force the ones that don't feel right. Instead, come back to those ideas later, and you might interpret them in another way that seems more helpful. As my teacher Thich Nhat Hanh often says, we are just playing with these concepts, so try not to be caught by them.

The core message of this chapter is that all self-compassion practices can arise naturally out of the therapeutic relationship, rather than from rigidly following a script. Both psychotherapy outcome research and Buddhist psychology emphasize the importance of building a compassionate alliance between therapist and client.[1] This alliance becomes the foundation for everything that follows. As we start to incorporate self-compassion practices into our work, they can be a natural extension of our desire to understand our clients' suffering and support their well-being. A focus on alliance building is the first step toward effectively integrating self-compassion practices into therapy.

This chapter begins with a discussion of the role of alliance, then offers seven basic clinical principles to guide self-compassion work, and concludes with an introduction to Dialogue-Based Mindfulness, a new form of teaching mindfulness and compassion practices from a more relational perspective.

ALLIANCE, ALLEGIANCE, AND ADHERENCE

Psychotherapy outcome researchers such as Bruce Wampold, author of *The Great Psychotherapy Debate* (2013), generally agree about which elements of therapy are most important for creating real change. The therapeutic alliance that is built between the therapist and client is by far the most powerful factor, and is responsible for up to 60% of what makes therapy effective. I'll define what these researchers mean by *alliance* in more detail later in this chapter.

The second most important factor is what researchers call *allegiance*, which is responsible for about 30% of outcome. An example of someone with low allegiance would be a therapist who has been trained in Gestalt and Hakomi methods, but is hired by an agency that requires her to use cognitive–behavioral therapy (CBT) with all of her clients. It's not her favorite orientation and she'd rather be working in a different way, so we can say she has low allegiance to the CBT interventions she's using. Researchers have found that it's important to use techniques you believe in and that make sense to you.

Finally, researchers use the word *adherence* to refer to how closely therapists stick to a manualized treatment. Are they doing exactly what is written up or what makes the most sense to them? It turns out that rigidly trying to adhere to a treatment protocol is not very helpful in therapy. When researchers look at the numbers, they find that how closely therapists follow the exact details of an intervention matters very little in terms of how much the client benefits. This means that working in a way that feels authentic to us as therapists and flows from our compassion for our clients is going to be much more effective than trying to be technically precise in the way we implement a certain intervention.

When we really let the meaning of this research in, it can be a welcome relief. Although many people try to convince us that it is extremely important to follow *their* protocols exactly, this is just not supported by research. The message to all of us is that when we are learning a new technique, we can feel free to adapt other people's work so that it feels authentic to us. It's not the specific details of the intervention that matter as much as the fact that we believe in what we are doing and have built a strong alliance with our clients.

BUILDING A COMPASSIONATE ALLIANCE

When researchers say that the therapeutic alliance is the most important factor in successful therapy, what exactly do they mean? Psychotherapy outcome researchers talk about three core elements of a strong alliance: shared goals, a shared understanding of what is going to help, and the quality of the bond between therapist and client.

Setting Shared Goals

Let's start by looking at goals. When I offer trainings for therapists, I ask people to bring up their most difficult clients, and we explore how self-compassion practices could be helpful. I'd say about half of the clients that people bring up don't have severe symptoms or issues that are very complex. Instead, they are clients who aren't fully engaging with therapy or have been resisting some of the therapist's efforts. A recent example was from a psychiatrist named Beth who brought up her client, Neal, a middle-age man who spent nearly every session complaining about the people in his life. Beth said, "I listen and I want to help, but we aren't really getting anywhere, and I've been seeing this guy for over a year. Do you think self-compassion might help him?"

When I heard her description, I wasn't trying to diagnose Neal or think about how the kind of resilience and optimism that come from self-compassion would make his life better. Instead, I was just wondering what Neal wants from therapy. Why does he keep showing up, especially if his psychiatrist thinks they aren't getting anywhere? I know that building an alliance with Neal is extremely important and that agreeing on goals is a vital part of the therapeutic alliance. I'm completely open to the possibility that Neal might just want someone to listen to him. His goal might be nothing more than getting a little empathy once a week. If that is the case, however, I'd want to make sure he's experiencing the relationship as empathic, and that he knows the invitation is open if he decides he wants to work on changing something in his life.

I asked Beth, "If you were to ask Neal why he keeps coming to therapy, what do you think he would say?"

She responded, "He says a lot of people told him he should go to therapy, so that must mean he needs it." Everyone at the training laughed, because we've all been in this situation. However, this answer also did a lot to explain why Beth was having such a hard time with this client. More than a year into therapy, she still didn't really understand Neal's deeper goals and motivations. I asked if Beth would be willing to do a role-play in which she would play Neal and I would play the therapist. She agreed, and this is how it went:

TIM [*as therapist*]: Hi, Neal. So I thought maybe we could start today taking a little time to look at what you really want from therapy. I'd like to make sure we're working on what matters most to you.

BETH [*as Neal*]: Yeah, it's like I said. People tell me I should see a psychiatrist, so I must need it. I don't know. What do you think?

TIM: I don't know. You say you're here because other people told you it would help. I guess I'm wondering how we would know if it's actually helping. Is there anything in your life that you would like to be different?

BETH: Oh, my God, yeah. Can you make my wife stop bothering me, and my boss stop being such a jerk, and my neighbor clean up his lawn? I've got a list, Doc. I could go on. You know this.

TIM: Yeah, we've talked about that. (*short pause*) I want you to know I really wish I *could* do those things. If I could make those people treat you better, I would. (*Short pause to let that sink in.*) The problem is that none of them is here in this room.

BETH: Yeah, that's what I'm saying! (*laughs*)

TIM: I know. We both wish we could somehow make those people change, but we don't have that power. So what I'm wondering is whether there might be some way that *you* could change, or some skill you could develop that might make dealing with these people a little less painful.

BETH: That would be great. What do you have in mind?

TIM: Let's pick one of those hard relationships and look at it to see if we can come up with something.

We continued the role-play and Neal chose his wife. He described an experience in which he was watching TV when his wife got home, and she began berating him about not helping enough with the housework. I asked, "If you had something you could do, right in that moment, that would make this experience less painful, would that be worth working on?" His answer was an emphatic "Yes," and now we had a real shared goal. We ended the role-play there, and Beth expressed how helpful it had been for her. She had been trying her best to help, but it wasn't very effective because she had missed this crucial step of agreeing on a goal.

Let's go back over that role-play so that I can explain what I was thinking. We started off with an exchange I believe Beth had had with the real Neal in the past: I asked about his goals, and the response was that he didn't know.

Beth had mentioned that he would complain a lot about problems in his life, so it's clear that he's suffering. However, he talked about his problems as though they were completely external, and he didn't seem to see how he could do anything to make them any better. When he gave me that list of people he wished would change, I took the opportunity to express my honest compassion for him rather than telling him to take more responsibility in those relationships. He was basically saying, "I wish the people in my life were kinder and more considerate to me," and I could honestly agree with him. I essentially said, "I wish that too." We were both wishing him happiness, and that was an important moment of alliance building. However, please don't assume that I believe this is the "only right way" to respond to a client like Neal. This is just *one* way to build a compassionate alliance.

At that point, I could have waited for Neal to recognize that we don't have the power to change other people. However, since it was a 5-minute role-play, I decided to move things forward and bring up the possibility that there might be some skill he could develop that would make these problems less painful. I didn't try to convince him that there definitely is, because he might not be willing to take that on faith. I said, "If we *could* find something like that, would it be worth our time?" In that moment, I wanted to get us on the same team. It worked, and our shared goal became exploring whether there might be something Neal could do to suffer less in these difficult relationships. With a shared goal established, let's take this example forward and look at the next element of alliance building.

What Will Help?

Let's imagine this session with Neal continuing. He had just told me the story of his wife yelling at him about housework, and he agreed that if there were some way to make this ordeal less painful, that would be great. At that point, I'd want to get more details about his emotional reaction when she was yelling at him, because I'd want to be able to put myself in his shoes as much as possible. I cover this aspect in more detail later in this chapter, but for now, my point is that being able to personally relate to the client's experience can be extremely helpful in creating appropriate interventions.

Neal might say something like, "As soon as she looked at me with that angry look in her eyes, it's like I panic. I'm already panicking before she even says anything." He describes getting extremely emotionally agitated in these kinds of situations and that his agitation causes him to speak or act in ways that make the problem worse. Once I understand this, I think that he might benefit from learning some tools for emotional regulation and self-soothing, such as mindfulness of the body (which I cover in Chapter 4). I lead him through a mindfulness exercise, and he reports that it calms him a lot. Just to double-check, I ask, "Do you think that this kind of practice might be able to help you in stressful situations with your wife?" He agrees and now we have a real plan.

The first part of creating a compassionate alliance was agreeing on an initial goal: Find something that could help Neal experience these conflicts with less suffering. We now have completed the second part, which is agreeing on a plan that makes sense to both of us. We are both optimistic that learning and practicing mindfulness of the body could help Neal self-soothe in moments of conflict with his wife. Now the task before us becomes helping him develop that ability.

The concept I want to emphasize here is that this intervention came naturally out of the process of developing an alliance. We clarified his goals and then explored what we could do that might help him accomplish them. The plan we created to help Neal learn mindfulness of the body was entirely based on the clinical goals we had created together. As you move forward with learning the techniques and practices in this book, they will work best if they are rooted in a strong therapeutic alliance.

Warmth and Empathy

Ever since Carl Rogers published "The Necessary and Sufficient Conditions for Therapeutic Personality Change" in 1957, our field has understood that empathy, understanding, and positive regard are vital elements of psychotherapy. Outcome researchers call these *common factors* because they are valued by every therapeutic tradition and orientation. Sadly, our field tends to focus more on the differences between schools of therapy rather than emphasizing the factors that *we all agree are important*. This can lead to some of the most important elements of therapy being overlooked.

> ***Sadly, our field tends to focus more on the differences between schools of therapy rather than emphasizing the factors that we all agree are important.***

The word *compassion*, as defined in Chapter 1, is an excellent way of expressing the emotional tone of a successful therapeutic relationship. Compassion includes the elements of empathy, understanding, and positive regard. We comprehend the person's suffering and what is causing that suffering (understanding); we can deeply connect with the person's experience (empathy); and we wish them wellness and relief from suffering (positive regard).

Generating the feeling of compassion is the third core element of building a strong therapeutic alliance. Yet, although most therapists would agree on the importance of having compassion for clients, there is very little discussion about how to get better at cultivating that feeling.

How can we develop our ability to generate compassion? As I described in Chapter 1, one of the most powerful tools I've found for strengthening and developing compassion is a concentrated self-compassion practice. When I apply the techniques described in Chapters 4–8 on myself, it becomes so much easier to feel compassion for even my most difficult clients. I believe that committing ourselves to developing self-compassion is the greatest gift we can give our clients and ourselves.

Seven Principles for Integrating Self-Compassion into Your Work

Now I'll highlight a handful of principles that I hope will help make it easier for you to begin to incorporate self-compassion practices into your work.

1. *Connect with the client's goals.* Many clients come into therapy with clear goals like feeling less anxious or depressed. Some, like Neal, come to therapy willingly but can't articulate their goals. With this group, I suggest taking the time to help them explore their own motivations for coming to therapy and the problems they want to address (as in the example above).

   Even mandated clients have goals that we can share. A common one is to be released from your program. When I'm trying to connect with a mandated client, I will often use a question such as "How would you like things to be different in your life?" to help them begin to identify a goal on which we could work. In the rare event that a mandated client says there is nothing he or she would like to be different, I usually just say, "OK, then what do you want to do for the next 50 minutes?" I find that if I set the agenda for a client without his agreement, I'm giving him something to resist. By refusing to set the agenda, I communicate to clients that I'm just here to help them as much as possible with whatever problem they identify in their lives. I find this attitude makes it more likely that the client will set the agenda.

2. *Maintain the motivational boundary.* What I call the *motivational boundary* involves accepting clients exactly as they are, but still being very happy to help them change. In other words, I'm really motivated to help a client change *only because* he or she has expressed wanting to change *and* wanting my help. If I notice that I want the client to change *for my own reasons* or more than they do, I consider that crossing the motivational boundary and a big mistake. In general, if I'm exhausted at the end of a session, it's usually because I crossed the motivational boundary and was trying to moti-

vate an ambivalent client. When I stay on my side of the boundary, sessions are usually pretty pleasant.

3. *Improvise and experiment.* Since we know that rigidly trying to adhere to manualized treatments or follow scripts is not associated with better outcomes, *but* using interventions that make sense to us is, we can feel free to be creative and experiment. With a client like Neal, we can begin by connecting with his goal and then coming up with a shared understanding of what might help him. When we agree he might benefit from using mindfulness to self-soothe during conflicts with his wife, the next question would be: How do we teach him to do that?

In my years of experience teaching mindfulness and self-compassion, one of the biggest lessons I've learned is that if I give the same meditation instructions to different people, they will respond differently. I have to be willing to change and adapt my instructions based on how the client is responding. The principle of Dialogue-Based Mindfulness, which I explain below, provides a technique for assessing how a client is responding to our guidance.

In Buddhist psychology, there is a strong emphasis on the uniqueness of the individual. At a recent lecture at Harvard, the Dalai Lama was asked to lead a guided meditation for the group of people assembled. He refused, explaining that the people in the audience are dealing with different obstacles and have different strengths, so it wouldn't make sense to give them all the same meditation instructions (as cited in Pollak, Pedulla, & Siegel, 2014). Thich Nhat Hanh also says that one of the foundational principles of his teaching is for people to experiment with practices for themselves, and that the only way to know if you are practicing correctly is if the result is less suffering and more happiness (Hanh, 1998). If something isn't clicking, we just change it and see if that works better. My hope is that this book will give you all of the instructions you need to guide clients through many different mindfulness and self-compassion practices.

4. *Be authentic.* Rather than trying to imitate an expert, each of us can do our best to understand our clients' suffering, its causes, and what might help. We use interventions that make sense to us, often based on our own practice of mindfulness and self-compassion. We don't have all the answers, but we are deeply committed to bringing our own life experience and training to help as much as we can. We will not always understand the client's experience, but we want to, so we give ourselves permission to be curious and ask questions.

5. *Empathy: Putting ourselves in the client's shoes.* As we begin to explore mindfulness and self-compassion in our own lives, we get to know ourselves a lot better. We become more aware of our own feelings, even very subtle ones, as they come and go. We also become more confident in our ability to calm and soothe our negative emotions. This process helps deepen our capacity for empathy because we can relate more easily to a client's experience. In my own life, I know what it feels like to be angry, terrified, hopeless, lonely, etc. I have also had the opportunity to practice sending compassion to those feelings and have a lived experience of being able to comfort them. So when a client says he or she is terrified about a big performance or feeling hopeless about recovering from depression, I can honestly say to myself, "Oh, hopelessness. I know that feeling, and I know we can learn to take care of it." I feel a strong sense of hope and self-efficacy that the client can perceive.

Thich Nhat Hanh often says that the Buddha was a normal human being who still suffered. The difference was that he had learned how to take care of his suffering and embrace it so he was never caught by it. Suffering could arise in him, and he would immediately send it compassion until it resolved.

A common mistake is to believe that we understand what a client is experiencing before we really do. If a client says she is "depressed," do we really know what she means by that? Is she grieving a loss, hating herself, or just feeling lethargic? If another client says he is "scared about moving to Florida," does that mean he is afraid of not finding a job and becoming homeless, that he will miss his extended family, or that this move is something he has built up in his mind as the solution to all of his problems and he's afraid that he'll be disappointed? I believe an important part of *accurate empathy* is not assuming we understand the other person's experience too soon. Instead, we let ourselves be curious about all the nuance and details of each client's experience.

6. *Our own practice is our best guide.* Some people say that it's impossible to use mindfulness or self-compassion with clients unless you practice those things yourself. I don't believe this is true. There are plenty of therapists who use these techniques without ever having formally practiced them. However, I do believe that the greatest gift we can offer our clients and ourselves is to develop our own practice of mindfulness and self-compassion. As we learn to practice self-compassion, we not only have an easier time feeling compassion for others. Practicing on ourselves is also the absolute best way to develop confidence in creatively adapting these techniques for different situations. We will inevitably find that a particular technique can feel powerful one day and lifeless the next. As we accrue more and more hours devoted to these practices, we develop a familiarity with how obstacles arise within ourselves and how they can dissolve when met with compassion. This will be the focus of Chapter 11.

7. *Have the client experience a practice before you explain it.* Some of my clients come to see me because they want to learn self-compassion and they know that is my specialty. However, most of them are coming to therapy because they are depressed, anxious, or having a relationship problem. Unless a client specifically wants to learn about meditation, I will almost never use the words *meditation*, *mindfulness*, or *self-compassion* until I've already guided them through that kind of practice and they've experienced some benefit. I

don't want the words to become an obstacle since some clients have preconceived notions about whether these practices could really help them.

With every client, I begin by clarifying our shared goals. If a client's goal is to feel less anxious in social situations, I might say, "Would you be willing to try an exercise to see if we can understand your anxiety a little better?" or "Can we try a practice to see if it might help you feel less anxious?" Most clients will just say "Yes," and I will guide them through a mindfulness or self-compassion exercise. I find that this makes things much easier than trying to explain these concepts before a client has any lived experience of them. If a client responds to my question by saying, "That depends—what do you have in mind?" I'm not secretive at all. I explain the practice as clearly as I can. However, most clients will just agree to try the practice, so I can jump into the intervention and explain it only after they have experienced the benefit. You will see more examples of how I do this later in the book.

The purpose of all these principles is to help you integrate self-compassion practices into your work in a way that feels as authentic as possible. As they say in 12-step communities, "Take what you like and leave the rest."

DIALOGUE-BASED MINDFULNESS

As I mentioned earlier, people respond in their own unique ways to guided meditations. I often begin group trainings by leading everyone in a simple practice of mindful breathing that focuses on enjoying the sensation of the breath. At the end, I ask about how different people experienced that exercise. It is common for one person to say that being instructed to enjoy the breath made the exercise extremely pleasant and it was one of the best meditation experiences she had ever had. However, another person might say that his breathing felt constricted and he felt guilty or ashamed that he wasn't able to enjoy it. Using the same guidance, one person ended up feeling wonderful and the other person felt horrible.

It is for this reason that I developed Dialogue-Based Mindfulness (DBM), which helps us to change and adapt meditation instructions depending on how the client responds. It is a general principle that I use with all of the specific techniques in this book.

In the more traditional way of leading guided meditations, the person leading the practice gives instructions and the person or people who are learning remain silent. This is a form of teaching that is excellent for silent retreats and people who are practicing more advanced stages of mindfulness. However, in DBM, the client gives the therapist verbal feedback about his or her experience *during the exercise*. The therapist uses this feedback to adjust and custom-tailor the meditation instructions in order to ensure that the client learns the technique effectively.

Here is an example of how DBM might look in a session that's focused on teaching mindfulness of the body to calm performance anxiety.

THERAPIST: Would you be willing to try an exercise to see if it might help when you need to perform and are feeling anxious?

CLIENT: Sure, if you think it might help.

THERAPIST: It might. Let's see. (*pause*) Let's start by picturing yourself just before a performance, and let me know when you feel like you're really there.

CLIENT: (*Closes eyes.*) I'm there.

THERAPIST: Great. Seeing all those people in front of you, what are the sensations you notice in your body? Is there tension, relaxation, heaviness, or lightness? Anything like that?

CLIENT: Well, my chest is really tight and my whole body feels like it's shaking.

THERAPIST: Perfect, thanks. (*slowly*) So there is tightness in your chest and your whole body feels shaky. (*pause*) Now let's see if it's possible for you to just let those sensations be there in your body without trying to change them at all. See if you can, for a minute or so, let yourself just feel that tightness in your chest and shakiness in your body.

CLIENT: It doesn't feel good. It's pretty intense.

THERAPIST: That's OK. That's perfect. You're doing it. So even though it feels really unpleasant, you are just letting that tightness in your chest and shakiness be there in your body. Just feeling them and not trying to make them go away.

CLIENT: (*Eyes still closed.*) I want them to go away.

THERAPIST: Yes. That's totally fine. It's OK to want them to go away. Just let yourself feel all of it. The tightness in your chest and the shakiness are there. And the feeling that you want them to go away is also there. We are letting all of those things be true in this moment. See if you can let them all be there and feel them.

CLIENT: Yeah, I can. It's not easy, but I can.

THERAPIST: Great. (*pause*) As you are staying with all of these feelings in your body, let me know if they get stronger or change in any other way.

CLIENT: I guess they are getting weaker, but they are still there.

THERAPIST: Great. Remember, we aren't trying to make them go away. We are just learning that we can feel them and tolerate them. They might get stronger, and that's OK, or they might continue to relax. We are just watching.

CLIENT: Yeah. They are really relaxing. I feel like just not fighting them helps them to relax. I feel better.

In Chapter 4, I explore mindfulness of the body in a lot more depth, but for now I just want to emphasize the important role of two-way communication in this exercise. If I hadn't asked the client to report his experience to me, I wouldn't have known when he started thinking "I don't like these feelings." It's really likely that he would have gotten stuck there and decided this practice didn't work for him. That thought would have just played over and over in his head, and he would have stopped following my instructions. Instead, I was able to guide him through that obstacle (I explain how in Chapter 4), and he ended up having a really positive experience.

I believe that DBM is a more effective way to teach mindfulness and self-compassion to a clinical population for three reasons. First, our clients deal with a lot of mental obstacles when attempting these practices. This client could have easily gotten stuck in a negative thought pattern if I weren't able to track him. In the mindfulness of breathing example from earlier, I mentioned that it's fairly common for even simple meditation instructions to trigger shame, self-criticism, or anxiety. DBM allows therapists to monitor these potential pitfalls and guide clients to safety.

The second reason is that our clients are much more likely to give up on a practice if they don't find real benefit right away. The more traditional way of learning mindfulness and self-compassion requires a lot of persistence and willingness to sit through (seemingly) unproductive meditation sessions. However, I've found I can often help a client experience real benefit from these practices in our first session using DBM.

Finally, it just works. Having to verbally describe one's experiences during a meditation session is not appropriate for advanced meditators when they are working with more subtle levels of thought, feeling, and perception. When the mind is very peaceful, it is distracting to have to verbalize anything. However, therapy clients are mainly dealing with strong emotions and loud, persistent thoughts. Having worked with thousands of clients and therapists using this method, I've found that DBM can be enormously helpful in these kinds of situations.

As we explore integrating self-compassion as a core focus of therapy, we will be guided by the principles of building a strong therapeutic alliance and using dialogue in order to better guide clients through meditation exercises.

Chapter 4

MINDFULNESS OF THE BODY

Techniques for Building Affect Tolerance and Regulation

"Mindfulness is not a tool. It is a path."
—Thich Nhat Hanh

I came to Buddhist meditation as a 20-year-old young man with a lot of sadness and anger from a difficult childhood. When I first encountered Thich Nhat Hanh's teachings, I embraced them wholeheartedly, often spending months at a time on meditation retreats with him. To this day, I try to spend at least 60 days on retreat each year, including a day of mindfulness every Sunday at Morning Sun Mindfulness Center, in Alstead, New Hampshire, where I live.

Buddhist meditation has been one of the greatest gifts in my life. Through these practices, I have been able to develop more happiness and inner peace than I would have thought possible, and it is because of my own personal experience, as well as my experience with clients, that I feel confident in saying that psychotherapy is only beginning to scratch the surface of what Buddhism has to offer.

I believe that the explosion of interest in mindfulness in our field, as well as in other helping professions, scientific research, and popular culture, is just a beginning. There is so much more we can learn from these practices about how to relieve suffering and cultivate well-being, as well as how to create more harmony in our relationships and develop a deeper sense of meaning in our lives.

However, as the influence of mindfulness expands in our culture, we are also finding that less qualified teachers are portraying themselves as experts in mindfulness. They present an impoverished notion of mindfulness that is not connected to the depth of tradition that makes true mindfulness so powerful. This phenomenon, sometimes called *McMindfulness*, has the potential to undermine the good that authentic teachers could create in the world. I believe it is important to be careful in selecting mindfulness teachers and to familiarize ourselves with the traditional Buddhist teachings from which these practices come.

WHAT IS MINDFULNESS?

If you were to attend a public talk by Thich Nhat Hanh or the Dalai Lama, you might hear something like, "Mindfulness is just paying attention to the present moment," or "Mindfulness is bringing your awareness to the here and now." This is true, but there is also a lot more to it. If you were to continue studying with either of those teachers, you would be given more and more specific, detailed, and nuanced instructions about exactly *what kind of awareness* mindfulness is and exactly how we can cultivate it.

One of the core analogies that Thich Nhat Hanh uses to describe mindfulness is of a mother holding her newborn baby—that kind of open, loving, accepting awareness. When we bring mindfulness to our breathing, our fear, or any other object, we don't just watch it in a way that is emotionally flat or cold, nor are we merely "nonjudgmental." There is a kind of tenderness and open-heartedness that is vital to the practice of true mindfulness. Take a moment and see if you can connect with that energy in yourself.

This way of construing mindfulness is not unique to Thich Nhat Hanh. It is fundamental to how the term is understood in every traditional school of Buddhist psychology. In the original collection of Buddhist teachings (the *Pali Canon*), the main treatise on Buddhist psychology, the *Abhidhamma*, defines mindfulness as having 18 necessary characteristics, which include love, generosity, and respect.[1] In other words, if our mindfulness doesn't have warmth and tenderness, it isn't real mindfulness.

Another essential aspect of mindfulness is what Buddhists call *Right View*. When we practice mindfulness or compassion, our practice is informed by how we understand the world. If our worldview is materialistic and individualistic, then that will color our mindfulness practice in a way that is different than if our worldview were based on interdependence.

Different schools of Buddhism explain Right View differently, but all of them emphasize that our basic worldview is the foundation upon which our meditation practices are built. Thich Nhat Hanh often says, "If you are practicing mindfulness without Right View, then you are practicing Wrong Mindfulness."

If Right View is so important, then what is it and how does it relate to therapy? Every school of Buddhism teaches that nothing is fundamentally separate or disconnected from anything else.[2] If you think about the piece of paper from which you are reading right now, it might seem like nothing special. However, we all know that it used to be a part of a tree. Without that tree, the paper couldn't exist. Thich Nhat Hanh would say the tree is present in the paper if you look deeply.

The tree was made out of soil, sun, and rain. Without any of those things, the tree couldn't exist, so they are present in the paper as well. At some point the tree was cut down and brought to a factory, so without those workers and all their ancestors, it could never have become paper. If we continue this line of thought, very quickly we can see that everything in the universe has had some role in bringing this paper into existence. One of the most common expressions of Right View is that, at the most fundamental level, we are deeply interconnected with everything in the universe.

You might ask, "How does this pertain to my work with clients?" I almost never try to explain Right View to a client. However, it definitely informs a great deal of what I do with them. From the perspective of Right View, our suffering is not ours alone. It comes to us from many different causes and conditions. The anxiety in you might have come from your mother's anxiety.

Her anxiety might be the product of growing up without enough food to eat or from her grandfather's trauma in World War I. Some therapists attempt to help their clients stop blaming themselves for their suffering by encouraging them to blame their parents. However, we know that our parents didn't ask for their suffering either. Right View is connected to compassion because we see that *there is no one to blame*. The suffering of the world belongs to all of us, and we all share responsibility for transforming it.[3]

HOW DO WE PRACTICE MINDFULNESS?

There is a saying that the Buddha taught 84,000 different kinds of meditation. That's not meant to be a literal number, but to convey that different meditation instructions are appropriate for different people in different moments of their lives. If you are looking for a one-size-fits-all approach, you won't find it here. However, if you can embrace the understanding that mindfulness practice is a creative and constantly changing process, the benefits are limitless.

As I mentioned in Chapter 3, being willing to improvise and experiment is absolutely essential for cultivating mindfulness. Rather than rigidly trying to follow one specific set of instructions, we can familiarize ourselves with many different ways of meditating and creatively experiment to find something that works for us in a particular moment. In mindfulness-based therapy, we are trying to help our clients develop beneficial states of mind, and, as I mentioned earlier, the only way to know whether they are practicing correctly is by the fact that they are experiencing less suffering and more happiness.

This means that there isn't a "right" or "wrong" way to guide someone in mindfulness practice. What matters is that your instructions actually help clients *experience* beneficial states of mind. There is a very popular parable in Buddhism from the Surangama Sutra that likens the Buddha's teachings to a finger pointing at the moon. The entire purpose of the finger is to get you to look at the moon and experience it for yourself. If you stare at the finger instead of the moon, you miss the point.

It is the same way with therapists and clients. If we help our clients connect with the healing energy of mindfulness and compassion, through our modeling and our instructions, we have done our job. If we give instructions but the client is not experiencing any benefit—even if we are doing exactly what "an expert" taught us to do—we must change the instructions until we are successfully able to *point the client* in the direction of mindfulness.

GETTING THE MOST FROM SESSION TRANSCRIPTS

For the rest of the book, I'm going to be using a lot of word for word transcripts of therapy sessions as a way to demonstrate exactly how these teachings and practices can be implemented in your work with clients. I believe these transcripts may be the most helpful resource for actually developing comfort and confidence in using these practices.

In my experience of training therapists, I have found that sharing actual examples is the most effective way of communicating principles so that people can put them into practice in a creative, natural way. I suggest reading them several times. I also suggest the following exercise as a way to help you get the most benefit out of these transcripts: Begin by covering the transcript with a piece of paper and moving it down one line at a time so that you can't see what happens next. When you read the client's line, stop and ask yourself why he or she might have said that and what you would have said in response. Then move the paper down to read what I said and compare it to what you would have said. Why did I say that? Why would you have said something different? I believe this process of slowing down and reflecting will help you learn much more.

You might decide that you prefer your response to mine, and that's totally fine. The important part is taking the time to ask yourself *why* I said what I said and reflecting on that *until it makes sense to you.* Don't move your piece of paper down to read the next line until you feel that you understand why I said what I said. Here is a summary of these instructions:

TRANSCRIPT EXERCISE

1. Cover the transcript with a piece of paper.
2. Read the client's line.
3. Why did the client say that?
4. What would you say in response?
5. Now read the therapist's line.
6. Why did the therapist say that?
7. Move on to the next line when you feel that you understand the therapist's response.

Example One: Karen the Psychologist

I begin a lot of my trainings by asking for a therapist to volunteer to be guided through a mindfulness of the body exercise. I like starting this way because it is generally much simpler than starting with a real client who would have more intense suffering and more obstacles that come up.

We'll look at a transcript from one such training. The volunteer is a psychologist named Karen who works part time at a prison and part time in private practice. After introducing herself, Karen said she had begun incorporating mindfulness into her work after attending a public talk by Thich Nhat Hanh and had had very mixed results. A couple of her clients took to the practice immediately and found it extremely helpful, while many others found attempting meditation frustrating or awkward. She said that she signed up for my training after reading that Thich Nhat Hanh is my core teacher, and she hoped to be able to find new ways to help more of her clients benefit from mindfulness practice.

I asked her to find a comfortable posture in her chair and, with her eyes opened or closed, to bring her awareness to all of the sensations in her body and let me know what she finds there.

KAREN: (*With her eyes closed, after a short pause.*) Hmm. I'm noticing tightness in my shoulders. My belly feels a little heavy after a big breakfast, and a little tingling in my hands and feet. I guess I'm a little nervous with everyone watching me.

THERAPIST: (*Speaking very slowly with long pauses between sentences; imagining feeling the sensations she describes and embracing them with mindfulness.*) Good. Thanks. Now just let yourself feel all of that without trying to change it at all. You can feel the tightness in your shoulders, the heaviness in your belly, and the tingling in your hands and feet. Just let it be there and let yourself feel it. It might get stronger or change in some other way. Let me know if it changes at all.

KAREN: (*Eyes still closed after another short pause.*) Yes. Just as you said that, my shoulders began to relax, but I'm still feeling the tingling in my hands and feet.

THERAPIST: Good, good. Allow yourself to stay with that now. Let yourself feel your shoulders relaxing and the tingling in your hands and feet. We are not trying to change anything, just to feel whatever comes up. These sensations can come or go however they want to. Let me know if anything else changes.

KAREN: (*Takes a deep breath, pauses for a minute or so, and now broadly smiling.*) Yes. Now I just feel very comfortable and relaxed. My hands and feet feel warmer. It's like as soon as I gave myself permission to feel these things, they let go.

THERAPIST: Good. Let's take a few breaths and enjoy that sensation of warmth and relaxation. Allow yourself to really feel and enjoy those sensations in the body, but stay open to whatever else might want to come up. We'll take about five more breaths from this place.

As I mentioned, this is a very simple example with no big obstacles to overcome. Since most of your clients won't be this easy, we will explore more complicated cases as well.

I opened this exercise by asking Karen to notice all of the sensations in her body, and to report whatever she found. This is an example of Dialogue-Based Mindfulness (DMB) because I solicited verbal feedback from the client throughout the exercise.

WHAT IS MINDFULNESS OF THE BODY?

As you might have noticed, my main focus was to guide Karen to welcome and accept the sensations in her body as completely as possible. Through developing the ability to observe strong emotions with openness and acceptance, our capacity to tolerate them grows and our reactivity decreases. This is how mindfulness of the body leads to improved affect tolerance and regulation. Eventually, I would want to help Karen observe these sensations with the kind of warmth and tenderness I discussed earlier.

Although she mentioned feeling "a little anxious," I stayed focused on how that anxiety manifested in her body: namely, as tension in her shoulders and tingling in her hands and feet. Every strong emotion has physical sensations and thoughts associated with it. In my experience, focusing on the sensations in the body can help us stay grounded, like the trunk of a tree in a windstorm. Our thoughts might blow us all around, but the body can be a stable place to rest. We will explore practicing with thoughts in the next chapter.

When Karen reported an unpleasant sensation like tension, I told her that it's OK if that sensation gets stronger. Some clients will believe that you really want their negative feelings to go away, even if you're explicitly saying that you don't. When we tell them it's really OK for negative feelings to get stronger (or stay the same), it makes it clearer that we want them to observe their feelings and report back.

You might also have noticed that I responded, "Good" or "Yes" to whatever sensation she described. Through this kind of affirmation, I wanted to communicate that she had followed the directions and that the process was proceeding well. This is also a way of modeling open acceptance for whatever sensations arise. Even if the tension or tingling in her feet and hands got stronger, all I was asking her to do was to observe these things as sensations in her body.

Although mindfulness of the body can create real healing and transformation, if a therapist is too focused on change, he or she will have a harder time modeling acceptance. We have to be willing to accept whatever comes up for our clients without any resistance in order to help them develop that ability. This is why I suggest that therapists think about mindfulness of the body in terms of developing affect tolerance. If we focus on training ourselves to be present with painful feelings in a way that isn't reactive, we can eventually develop the ability to observe our strong emotions with warmth and compassion.

You might also have noticed that I always repeated back the sensations Karen had just reported. My purpose was to keep her focused on those sensations, rather than spiraling off into her thoughts and losing touch with the body. Clients without much previous experience with meditation might lose focus in less than a minute if they aren't reminded to come back to their bodies.

Further, when she was experiencing positive feelings, I didn't just guide her to notice them and be indifferent. I encouraged her to *enjoy* them. It's important not to cling to positive affect states like relaxation and safety. We enjoy them while they are present, and then let them pass without grasping. In Buddhist psychology, positive feelings are viewed as an important source of energy. It's like positive feelings charge our batteries, and then we can use that energy to embrace and transform our suffering. In other words, effectively practicing with negative feelings requires that we have a reservoir of positive energy stored up, and that energy comes from moments of happiness.

Even in this simple example, we can see how adopting a stance of open acceptance can lead to healing and change. In my experience, about 75% of clients find that as soon as they are able to embrace their suffering with warmth and acceptance, they start to experience change right away. Like Karen said, when we give ourselves "permission to feel these things, they let go." Here is a brief summary of the important points:

MINDFULNESS OF THE BODY

- Emotions can be experienced as sensations in the body.
- Practice accepting bodily sensations as completely as possible.
- Positive feelings give us the energy needed to embrace and transform suffering.

Example Two: Calming Performance Anxiety

In Chapter 3, we considered an example of using DBM to calm performance anxiety. Let's look at that transcript again to highlight a few important concepts about mindfulness of the body.

THERAPIST: Perfect, thanks. (*slowly*) So there is tightness in your chest and your whole body feels shaky. (*pause*) Now let's see if it's possible for you to just let those sensations be there in your body without trying to change them at all. See if you can, for a minute or so, let yourself just feel that tightness in your chest and shakiness in your body.

CLIENT: It doesn't feel good. It's pretty intense.

THERAPIST: That's OK. That's perfect. You're doing it. So even though it feels really unpleasant, you are just letting that tightness in your chest and shakiness be there in your body. Just feeling them and not trying to make them go away.

CLIENT: (*Eyes still closed.*) I want them to go away.

THERAPIST: Yes. That's totally fine. It's OK to want them to go away. Just let yourself feel all of it. The tightness in your chest and the shakiness are there. And the feeling that you want them to go away is also there. We are letting all of those things be true in this moment. See if you can let them all be there and feel them.

CLIENT: Yeah, I can. It's not easy, but I can.

THERAPIST: Great. (*pause*) As you are staying with all of these feelings in your body, let me know if they get stronger or change in any other way.

CLIENT: I guess they are getting weaker, but they are still there.
THERAPIST: Great. Remember, we aren't trying to make them go away. We are just learning that we can feel them and tolerate them. They might get stronger, and that's OK, or they might continue to relax. We are just watching.
CLIENT: Yeah. They are really relaxing. I feel like just not fighting them helps them to relax. I feel better.

Although most clients experience immediate relief when they embrace their suffering with mindfulness, others (about 25%, in my experience) find that their negative feelings initially get stronger when they begin to focus on them. That was the case with this client. Unless we are dealing with acute trauma (which I cover in Chapter 9), the intensity will last only for a minute or so *if the client continues to bring open acceptance to the sensations*. In this example, it took just about 1 minute of nonresistance before the client's distress began to relax and transform.

The turning point in this session occurred when the client said that he wanted his feelings to go away. In that moment, I was faced with a choice of either ending the exercise or incorporating his aversion into it. Just like with any trauma protocol, including eye-movement desensitization and reprocessing (EMDR), Somatic Experiencing®, and exposure therapy, I was constantly assessing his level of emotional arousal. If he had crossed into a fight–flight–freeze state (which is evidenced by some physiological markers that we'll cover in Chapter 9), he would no longer be capable of effectively processing his emotions and I would definitely end the exercise and help him calm down.

In my experience of using this kind of guided mindfulness practice, most clients will open their eyes and "pop out" of the exercise before getting to such a level of overwhelm. In this example, the client wasn't showing any signs of hyperarousal. His eyes were still closed and he seemed to be concentrating on his internal experience. Although he said that he didn't want to connect with his painful feelings, I could see that he wasn't in danger of being overwhelmed.

Some clients will even say, "I can't do this—it's too much," while they are still completely immersed in the exercise. In cases like these, where the client is saying, "I don't like this," or "I can't do this," but is not exhibiting signs of hyperarousal, I will usually try to incorporate their expression of resistance into the exercise at least once, like I did here. I never oppose or argue against what the client says. I just comment that the thoughts they are experiencing *are thoughts*, and encourage the client to relate to those thoughts with the same openness and acceptance we are applying to the body. In this example, it worked really well, and the client's distress began to decrease almost immediately. However, if he had responded by saying, "No, I really don't want to do this," I would have stopped the exercise and talked about it with him.

I never want a client to feel pressured by me in any way, because I know that a compassionate alliance is so important. However, I will gently encourage clients to try to stay present with painful feelings, especially if we have agreed that doing so is important to their therapeutic goals.

Finally, when I use phrases like "see if you can" or "just for a minute," I'm trying to help the client experience my guidance as gentle suggestions, rather than as commands. I don't want anyone to feel pressured to perform, only encouraged to try.

Example Three: Social Anxiety and Addiction

Many therapists ask me how I explain mindfulness to clients before beginning these practices. As I mentioned in Chapter 3, the answer is that I usually don't. Since every intervention I use comes from the client's goals, I usually say something like this: "Would you be willing to try an exercise [or practice] to see if it might help your anxiety calm down [or might help us understand your depression, etc.]?" I've found that most clients are happy to try something without a detailed explanation if I present it like this.

However, the client in our next example, Laurel did want an explanation before trying something new. As you read the following transcript, notice how I initially transition into the exercise without explicitly talking about what it is. When she asks for an explanation, I comply immediately and only move on when I feel confident she is satisfied. Also notice how just accepting her feelings is not enough to create change (unlike the previous two clients), so I explicitly guide her to embrace them.

Laurel grew up in a middle-class family with very little emotional intimacy. Her parents divorced when she was young and although she excelled academically, she exhibited behavior problems as early as kindergarten. Laurel began using heroin in her early 20s. Since that time, she'd had some good years with a decent job and apartment, and some bad years that included prostitution and living in a shelter. She was 42 when she came to see me.

Her previous therapist, Gail, had referred her to me after about a dozen sessions that she felt were getting nowhere. She said that Laurel was highly noncompliant and would criticize any of her suggestions. This transcript is from our first session.

THERAPIST: Hi, Laurel. Gail told me a little about you, but I'd love to hear directly from you. What do you think is important for me to know about you? And what are your goals or hopes for therapy?

LAUREL: Well, I've been on and off methadone for a while now, and I'm trying to get my life straight. My daughter is always on my case about it, but she's a mess too, so she can't tell me anything. (*Visibly upset; looks down and pauses.*) Umm . . . I just need to stay clean, one day at a time. You know?

THERAPIST: Yeah. Let me know if I heard you right. (*slowly*) You really want to get clean and stay clean. That's the main thing right now. Your daughter gives you a hard time, and you try not to get too upset about it. But the main thing is staying clean. Did I hear you right?

LAUREL: Yeah. I just got to make good choices. Like, I picked up again this week [referring to heroin] and it threw me off. I had been doing OK, but then I picked up again. I hate myself when I do that (*more distressed*).

THERAPIST: So you picked up this week and you're regretting it? Is that what you're saying?

LAUREL: Yeah. I'm so sick of this (*more emotional*). It's like every time I get clean, I gotta go and screw it up. I wish there was some way to get me to think straight (*calms a little*). But I just gotta try again. You know, one day at a time.

THERAPIST: Yeah. It sounds like you really wish there were something that could help you stay sober. Is that right?

LAUREL: Absolutely. I'm sick of this. I don't want to keep living this way. I gotta get serious (*strong eye contact*). The problem is that nothing works. I'm a lost cause, so I'm not sure what you think you're going to do that's going to help me. I've tried everything (*pleading expression on her face*).

THERAPIST: OK. (*pause*) You really want to get clean, but everything you've tried hasn't helped. So I guess the question is whether we might be able to find something that could help you get clean and stay clean. Is that right?

LAUREL: Yeah, that would be great, but I don't think it's going to happen.

THERAPIST: Sure. It might not. I can't guarantee that we'll find something, but it sounds like it might make sense to use our time today and see if we can. I'd be happy if you just want to talk about yourself and your life, or if there are other things you'd like to talk about. However, if you want to, we can use this time to see if we can find a way to help you stay sober. It's up to you.

LAUREL: (*pause*) If there's something that could get me to stay sober, that's what I need. Let's do that.

THERAPIST: OK. (*pause*) Let's start by talking a little about the last time you picked up. That will help me understand what's getting in your way. Can you walk me through what happened?

LAUREL: Sure. I had an appointment at the methadone clinic, and I slept in a little and just couldn't get myself out of the door. So I missed it and I was hurting real bad, so I made the call and got some [referring to heroin].

THERAPIST: So you missed your appointment for methadone, and that led you to pick up again. (*pause*) You said you slept in a little and then couldn't get out the door. Can you tell me more about that?

LAUREL: Yeah. I mean I actually had time and stuff, but I kept thinking, I'm going to be late and the people there are going to be mad. Sometimes I just can't get out of the house. I don't know why.

THERAPIST: Is getting out of the house a big problem?

LAUREL: Oh my God, yes. I think that's my main problem. If I could just get myself out the door, I could do all the things the therapists tell me I need to do. I actually feel fine when I go out, but it's like I can't make myself do it.

THERAPIST: OK. Then let's pause and see if we can understand that a little better to see if we can find something that would help. Can you picture yourself that morning? It's after you woke up and you can't get yourself out of the house. Let me know if you can picture yourself back there.

LAUREL: Yeah. I'm there.

THERAPIST: OK, great. So right now picture that it's the time you know you'd have to leave your house to make the appointment, but you aren't leaving. Can you picture that?

LAUREL: Uggh. Yes. What's wrong with me?

THERAPIST: (*slowly*) We're going to slow down and look a little right here—right in that moment. It's the time you would have to leave your house to make the appointment—right there. Tell me what kinds of feelings you notice in your body. Is there any tension or relaxation, any heaviness or lightness? What do you notice there?

LAUREL: My whole body is tight like a fist, and I feel like I'm going to be sick. Wait. Why are we doing this? What are we doing?

THERAPIST: Oh, sure. You said getting out of the house is a big problem, so I'm trying to understand what makes it so hard to get out of the house. By imagining yourself right in that moment, we might be able to learn more about what's getting in the way. Does that make sense?

LAUREL: Sure. OK. Go ahead (*smiling; no nonverbal signs of reservation*).

THERAPIST: OK. So there you are, back on that morning. You have an appointment at the methadone clinic, and it's the time you'd need to leave your house to make it. Let me know when you're back there.

LAUREL: (*Eyes closed.*) I'm there.

THERAPIST: Now bring your attention to all the sensations in your body. You mentioned a tightness and feeling sick. Are those sensations still there?

LAUREL: Yeah, I feel horrible.

THERAPIST: (*pause*) Is there anything else, besides the tightness in your whole body and feeling sick in your stomach, that you notice?

LAUREL: (*pause*) No. That's it. My whole body feels balled up like a fist.

THERAPIST: OK. So now I'd like to see if it's possible, just for a minute, for you to *let yourself feel* all that tightness and that sick feeling in your stomach. Is it possible just to let yourself feel it without trying to make it go away?

LAUREL: No. It will take over. I can't.

THERAPIST: So you have a sense that those feelings will get stronger if you stop fighting them? Is that right?

LAUREL: (*Eyes still closed.*) Yes. I know they will. It's too much for me.

THERAPIST: OK. (*pause*) That makes sense. (*pause*) It's very possible that if you stop fighting these feelings, they will get stronger. However, I can see that even though they are really uncomfortable right now, you are tolerating them. You are strong enough to feel them. For a lot of people, if they stop fighting feelings like these, they get stronger for a minute or so, and then they start to feel better. So my question is whether you could try to see if that might happen to you. If you stop fighting these feelings for just a minute and see what happens.

LAUREL: OK. I'll try.

THERAPIST: OK. Now you are already feeling this intense tightness in your body and feeling sick in your stomach. See if you can, just for a minute, let yourself feel those feelings fully. Just let those feelings be there without trying to make them any different. They might get stronger, and that's OK. Let me know what you notice.

LAUREL: Yeah, they get stronger. The tightness is really intense and I feel like I'm going to throw up.

THERAPIST: OK, that's perfect. You are doing it. I can see that even though they are so strong, you can tolerate them. That's what we're learning now. So we're letting them be as strong as they want to be, and just feeling them. Let me know what you notice.

LAUREL: Yeah. It's just really intense. It's staying the same. It's my whole body.

THERAPIST: OK. Now see if it's possible to say to these intense feelings, "It's OK for you to be here. You can be as strong as you need to be. You are welcome."

LAUREL: I don't know if I can say that.

THERAPIST: Sure. No problem. There is a part of you that doesn't want these feelings. You can let yourself feel that too. Don't try to push that away either. The intense tightness and sick feeling are there, and the part of you that doesn't want to feel this is there too. See if you can say to all of it, "You are all welcome. It's OK that you're here."

LAUREL: (*pause*) Yeah, it relaxes. I feel a little like I want to cry, but in a good way.

THERAPIST: OK, stay with that. It might get stronger again, or it might keep relaxing. Either way is fine. Just let yourself feel it all and let me know what you notice.

LAUREL: (*pause*) Yeah, it feels a lot better. I'm not feeling sick and my body isn't so tense. It feels really good.

THERAPIST: OK. Let's take a few minutes to just enjoy feeling more relaxed and more comfortable. If the tightness wants to come back, that's OK. If it doesn't, you can just enjoy feeling relaxed.

LAUREL: Yeah, wow, it's such a huge relief. (*Crying gently.*) I can't remember the last time I felt like this.

After the exercise ended, we talked about how she could use this practice all the time. I explained that the more she practices this exercise when she's feeling OK or dealing with small negative feelings, the more likely it will be there for her when she's in crisis. This was certainly just a beginning for Laurel, but it was a good beginning. In the future, we would still need to look at the thoughts that were causing her distress (e.g., her fear of being late and people being mad) as well as other factors that contribute to her drug use. It's also very possible that she will have a hard time practicing on her own, and we might have to work on that as well.

Now let's go back through the transcript and look at a couple of important points. We all have different styles of building safety and rapport with new clients. Mine is to begin by getting as much clarity as possible about the client's goals as a way to build our alliance. There are about a dozen issues that Laurel brings up (her daughter, etc.) that I could have pursued, but I don't. They might all be really important, but I chose to stay focused on making sure I understood her goals, and I believe that ended up strengthening our relationship.

She conveyed that what was most important to her was to begin working on staying sober, so that's where we started. If she said she just wanted someone to listen to her talk about the problems in her life, we would have done that instead.

When Laurel expressed hopelessness, I didn't argue with her. I just reflected back the reality that she's tried many things and none seem to have helped. I also don't know for sure that what I will suggest is going to work. All we can do is try and see. I don't want to deny or invalidate her belief, but I also don't want to agree that her case is hopeless. Instead, I want to accept her and be present with her while she feels hopeless.

The second part of alliance building is about agreeing on *how* you will work toward the client's goal. At this point, I was wondering what obstacles were keeping her from sobriety, so I asked to hear the details of her most recent relapse. When she said she "couldn't get out the door," that made me curious and I decided to focus there. Why couldn't she get out of the door? What was stopping her? Although we might have answered that question only partially in the first session, a couple things became clear. She was feeling a lot of emotional distress, and she had isolated herself as a way of coping with it.

In order to explore what was keeping her from getting out the door, I guided her to picture herself right in the moment that she needed to leave. This is a technique with roots in Buddhism and neuroscience. A Buddhist teacher would say that in order to practice with a mental obstacle, we need to get in touch with it so that it is present in the body and mind. A neuroscientist would say that we could access much more information from an implicit memory when it is being activated.

For example, if I asked you, "How do you hold your thumb when you brush your teeth?" what would you have to do to get that information? Think about it for a moment. You would either imagine brushing your teeth or pretend to grip a toothbrush. If you had to answer that question without being able to do either of those things, you would only be able to guess. However, by pretending to grip a toothbrush, you can examine the position of your thumb with as much detail as you like.

Once Laurel was picturing herself in that critical moment, we had access to much more information about what was keeping her from being able to leave the house. Then the rest of the session focused on her learning how to cultivate open acceptance for those distressing sensations in her body.

She described a powerful tension in her whole body and feeling sick. When I first tried to help her embrace those sensations with mindfulness, she refused and said the feelings would take over if she stopped resisting them. I responded by acknowledging that she might be right. However, I also informed her that this intensifying usually lasts only a short time. I gently encouraged her to experiment and see if that would be the case with her.

Laurel ended up needing two adjustments to the original instructions before she started to experience relief. First, when she expressed not wanting to embrace her feelings, I guided her to welcome and embrace that aversion. Then I added the instruction to say explicitly, "You are welcome. It's OK you are here," to both her negative feelings and her aversion to those feelings. That helped her shift into a deep-enough level of open acceptance that she started feeling better. By the end of the session, she had a lived experience of the profound relief that can come from mindfulness practice. Now the next step will be helping her to use that practice instead of isolating herself and reverting to drugs. Following is a summary of this process.

MINDFULNESS OF DISTRESS IN THE BODY

1. Have the client visualize a scene that will activate the symptom; make sure it is present in the body and mind.
2. Have the client focus on the distress as sensations in the body.
3. Guide the client to practice open acceptance of the distress.
4. If the client experiences any resistance, guide him or her to accept the resistance and the distress.

TWO WAYS TO NAVIGATE

If you were to watch me guiding a client through mindfulness and self-compassion practices, you would see that my eyes are usually closed. As I'm working with clients or meditation students, I try to put myself in their shoes and go through the practice with them as much as possible. When a client says, "I can't handle this," I imagine having that thought myself. Putting myself in a client's shoes allows me to use my own experience with these practices as a compass to navigate.

As we deepen our own mindfulness practice, we become more and more comfortable with our own negative thoughts and feelings. I know what it's like to feel terrified, furious, and hopeless, and I've developed some confidence at being able to practice with each of those feelings. As I mentioned in Chapter 3, I believe developing our own practice of mindfulness and self-compassion is the single most helpful thing we can do for our clients.

However, it is possible to guide clients through these practices without having a great deal of personal experience by using "guess and check." You can try something and if it doesn't work, you just try something else.

Chapter 5

MINDFULNESS OF THOUGHTS
Techniques for Building Cognitive Flexibility

When Steven Hayes (2004), the co-originator of Acceptance and Commitment Therapy (ACT), talks about mindfulness of thinking, he talks in terms of three waves of psychology. Hayes comes from the cognitive–behavioral tradition, so the first wave in his model is behaviorism, which taught us how we can change behaviors by manipulating reinforcements: We reward some behaviors and not others, and watch how people (or pigeons) change. The second wave in Hayes's model is the cognitive revolution that brought about cognitive therapy and CBT. This radical shift taught us that if we change the thoughts that lead to behaviors, we could be more effective at changing those behaviors. However, anyone who has worked from a cognitive perspective knows that it isn't always as easy as it sounds. For example, if you are working with a client who is suffering from self-critical thinking, you might try to challenge those thoughts and offer more realistic assessments. Sometimes this can be extremely effective, but other times the negative thoughts just won't budge.

This brings us to the third wave in Hayes's model: mindfulness-based therapies. Hayes points out that if we can't always change the content of a thought, we often *can* change how we relate to it. The self-critical thought might continue to come up, but we learn to recognize that it's *just a thought*. We don't have to agree with it or argue against it. We can notice that it's only a thought and observe how it comes and goes. This way of relating to our thinking can create an experience of spaciousness and cognitive flexibility. We are no longer at the mercy of every thought that pops into our heads. Thoughts come and go, and we have the ability to observe them and reflect on which ones seem credible. Aristotle said that the mark of an intelligent mind is "to be able to entertain a thought without believing it" (Bennion, 1959, p. 52). That is what we practice when we engage in mindfulness of thinking.

RELATING TO OUR THOUGHTS

Most of us believe everything we think, which is kind of crazy. Looking back, it's easy to see that our thoughts are often mistaken. We thought someone at a party didn't like us or that the noise in our back yard was a bear, and it just wasn't true. However, somehow that doesn't stop us from believing whatever we happen to think next. It's like we can admit that a thought we had in the past wasn't totally accurate, but whatever we are thinking in the present just seems so absolutely real.

A more realistic perspective would recognize that most of our thoughts have some important kernel of truth, but are also distorted or limited in some way. Other thoughts might be completely delusional, and we can also have thoughts that seem to be a pretty accurate representation of how things are. Mindfulness of thinking helps us develop the ability to relate to our thoughts in this more realistic way, which can save us from a lot of unnecessary suffering.

Example One: Susan and the Furnace Guy

What does it mean to "observe our thoughts"? How is that different from the way we usually think? In my experience, it's much easier to convey what mindfulness of thinking means by looking at an example of it. The first example I share in this chapter comes from another training for therapists. Susan was a social worker who worked at a university hospital. When I asked for a volunteer to practice mindfulness of thinking, she raised her hand enthusiastically and said, "I think I need some of that."

I invited Susan to find a comfortable posture with her eyes open or closed, and to notice what thoughts were passing through her mind.

SUSAN: (*Eyes closed, speaking very quickly.*) The guy is coming to my house today to fix the furnace and my husband is supposed to be home, but he always screws things like this up, so I'm worried about that. And I'm thinking everyone here probably thinks I'm a bad person for saying that about my husband. Should I keep going?

THERAPIST: Great. Thanks. (*Pause; speaking slowly.*) See if you can just let those thoughts be there. You are wondering how things are going with your husband and the furnace guy, and you are wondering what the people here think about you. Just notice those thoughts are present in your mind. You don't know how things are going at home, and you don't know what people here are thinking about you. The mind *wants to know*, but it doesn't. (*pause*) When you let those thoughts be there, what sensations do you notice in the body?

SUSAN: Well, now I'm thinking that I really want to know how things are going at home. And I feel nervous about what people are thinking about me. I guess this whole exercise is making me really nervous. (*Eyes still closed; looks visibly tense.*)

THERAPIST: Great. That's perfect. (*pause*) See if you can just let yourself feel that nervousness without trying to make it go away. What does that feel like in your body?

SUSAN: My body feels tight, like a tightness in my chest, and I'm kind of getting a headache.

THERAPIST: OK. (*Speaking slowly.*) So even though it feels uncomfortable, see if you can just let yourself feel all of this without trying to make it go away. Just let yourself feel that tightness in your chest and the achiness in your head. Let them be as strong as they want to be. Let them come or go however they want. Let me know what you notice.

SUSAN: (*nervous tone in voice*) I just think that I don't want to feel those things. I don't think I'm doing this right.

THERAPIST: Great. Let those thoughts be there too. See if you can recognize these are also just thoughts. (*Susan smiles broadly, almost laughs; her eyes are still closed.*) There is a thought that you don't like to feel this discomfort, and there is a thought that you aren't doing the exercise right. It might be true or it might not, but we aren't worried about that now. (*pause*) See if you can just recognize that it's a thought without agreeing or disagreeing with it. These are just thoughts that pop into the mind. The physical discomfort is there and those thoughts are there too. We're just letting them all be there.

SUSAN: Yeah. Wow. (*Pauses, speaking much more slowly.*) I feel better. When you said that, it's like whatever I'm thinking is OK. Yeah, that tension is letting go a little. (*pause*) I feel like I'm doing it. I'm just watching my thoughts.

THERAPIST: Great. Perfect. Now, whatever thoughts pop into your mind are OK. You recognize they are just thoughts. Not identifying with them or arguing with them. You just let them be there and come back to the body. What are you noticing now?

SUSAN: My mind is quieter and I feel much better. I think this could be really helpful for one particular client.

THERAPIST: Notice that thought. (*She smiles again.*) There is the thought that this practice might help that client. We aren't agreeing or disagreeing with that thought, but just letting it be there.

SUSAN: Yeah. I'm thinking about my husband and work, but the thoughts are just coming and going on their own. It's like I'm not getting caught up in them. I'm just watching them. This feels really nice.

This example shows how negative reactions can be integrated into mindfulness practice to create a powerfully helpful result. Let's go back through the transcript from the beginning.

Susan is obviously nervous, and when she asks if she should keep listing her thoughts, I don't answer her explicitly. I mainly just want to slow her down. So I say thanks, and then pause for a few seconds. Then I give her some standard mindfulness of thinking instructions to see what she will do with them. I never know how a particular person is going to respond to a given set of meditation instructions so I said, "*See if you can* just let those thoughts be there." I wanted her to feel welcome to tell me if it wasn't working.

At that point Susan got really uncomfortable. She said the exercise was making her nervous, and it seemed like she was still fully identified with her thoughts. Although she seemed upset, I continued with the practice. There are times that it would make sense to end a practice like this if the client is getting overwhelmed or flooded. However, although she seemed distressed, I didn't think she was in danger of being overwhelmed, and she wasn't explicitly asking to stop. I was also aware that if I could help her embrace these difficult thoughts and feelings with mindfulness, it could be a powerful experience for her. So when she reported feeling nervous, I asked her to describe the physical sensations in her body.

As I mentioned in the last chapter, when someone describes an emotion, I think about it in terms of the sensations in the body and the thoughts/perceptions that go with those sensations.

In Buddhist psychology, there is no real correlate for our concept of emotions. What we call an emotion, say, anger, would be seen as a bodily state (e.g., tightness in the chest and jaw), a negative valence (i.e., it's an experience we don't like), and whatever thoughts or perceptions go with it (e.g., "That person is an idiot!"). In fact, Buddhist psychology categorizes anger (*pratigha*) as a mode of thinking (*caitasika*: mental factor). If you've seen "feelings" mentioned in Buddhist sutras, that's because the Pali word, *vedanā*, is often translated as *feelings*. However, since there are only three possible *vedanās*—positive, negative, and neutral—I believe the word would be better translated as *affective valence*. Some call it *feeling tone*. Although either term might seem a little abstract, the experience of exploring our emotions at this level of detail can be really clarifying.

When I asked Susan about the sensations in her body, she reported feeling tightness in her chest and a headache. At this point, it could be tempting to believe that this exercise wasn't going to work for her, but I could see that she hadn't yet shifted into an experience of open acceptance, and I was curious to see what would happen if she did. I have also experienced in myself and with many clients that sometimes a few rounds of negative thoughts will come up and have to be integrated into the practice before any magic happens.

I continued to affirm Susan's experience and gave her some simple instructions for mindfulness of the body. When I encouraged her to try accepting her feelings, she responded that she didn't want to. This was another point when I could have ended the exercise, but I didn't. Instead, I tried to guide her to accept those thoughts, as well. I described the reality that her uncomfortable feelings were present, and the thoughts about not liking those feelings and failing at the practice were also present. I encouraged her to try to accept all of it.

What happened next is actually fairly common. When she was instructed to accept and be present with the thought that she was failing at the exercise, a big shift occurred. In my experience, when people express the thought that a practice isn't working for them and are met with open acceptance from me (rather than agreeing or disagreeing), it can be surprising enough to shift them out of their habitual thinking. This seemed to be the case with Susan. After she said that she didn't think she was doing the practice correctly, I helped her recognize that this was just a thought as well. At that point, she was able to shift into the experience of watching her thoughts and described how these thoughts could come and go without disturbing her. Following is a summary of key points.

> ## MINDFULNESS OF THOUGHTS
>
> - If a client has negative thoughts about the exercise, they can be accepted and integrated into the practice.
> - Any emotion is made up of bodily sensations and thoughts/perceptions.

SUBJECT BECOMES OBJECT

One way that we can think about the practice of mindfulness, especially mindfulness of thinking, is in terms of how the subject of awareness becomes the object of awareness. This might sound somewhat mystical and complicated, but it's really not. When Susan first had the thought that she wasn't doing the exercise right, she was completely identified with that thought. Just a minute later, it was a thought that she was observing. It's like at first she was *in the thought,* and then she took a big step backward, metaphorically, so she could see the thought as an object in front of her. This is what it means for the *subject to become the object* in Buddhist psychology.

Example Two: Practicing with Anger

Now let's look at an example of this practice with a client. James originally came to see me for help in his relationship. He was very sensitive and whenever his girlfriend wasn't as tuned in to his needs as he wanted her to be, he would get angry. Our first few sessions focused on helping him communicate his needs in a way that was easier for his girlfriend to hear. He was getting better at being vulnerable, and it had helped a lot.

The session that we will look at now was the first one that wasn't focused on his relationship. He told me things were going much better in that part of his life, but he still lost his temper with other people and wanted to work on that.

THERAPIST: Can you walk me through a recent time you lost your temper with somebody and wished you hadn't?

JAMES: Sure. It was just 2 days ago. This guy that works at the dry cleaning place near my house is a complete jerk. I came in to pick up my dry cleaning, and it's not ready even though they guarantee that it will be done in 24 hours and it had been more like 36. So I say, "Why isn't it ready?" And he says (*in a sarcastic tone*), "Sorry man, it's not done. Do you want us to call you when it's ready?" And I'm like, "No, I want my laundry and it's supposed to be ready now." And it's like he was taking zero responsibility for screwing up (*sounding angry*), and I'm sick of it. So I started yelling at the guy and saying, "What are you going to do to fix this? This is your fault!" And he was just trying to brush me off and saying (*sarcastic tone*), "I can't do anything. What do you want me to do?" So I just lost it and started screaming at him and stormed out of there, and I was pissed off for the rest of the day.

THERAPIST: OK. Thanks. (*Pauses and takes a breath.*) So let me make sure I'm understanding you. Your laundry wasn't done and you got pissed off, right? Are you saying you'd like to be able to handle that differently?

JAMES: Well, I don't know because what are you supposed to do when someone treats you like that? (*Pauses and looks down.*) I don't want to be angry all the time, and Kelly [his girlfriend] says I overreact, but I refuse to be a doormat.

THERAPIST: So let me see if I'm hearing you right. You don't want to be getting angry all the time, and you also don't want to be a doormat. Is that right? So we are looking at whether it's possible for you not to be a doormat and still not get so angry.

JAMES: I guess. Yeah. (*Pauses and then speaks with decisiveness.*) Yeah. That's what I want.

THERAPIST: OK. Can we try an exercise to try to understand this situation a little better?

JAMES: Sure, whatever you think.

THERAPIST: OK. Can you picture yourself back there? You are

at the dry cleaners and you can see that guy. He just told you that your laundry isn't ready yet, even though it's been over 24 hours. Let me know when you can picture that.

JAMES: (*Eyes closed.*) Got it. I'm there.

THERAPIST: Great. Now let me know what feelings are coming up in your body. Is there tension, relaxation, heaviness, or lightness?

JAMES: My chest is really tight and so is my whole face. My hands are balling into fists, and I feel like I'm going to explode.

THERAPIST: Great. Perfect. Now see if it's possible, just for a minute, to let yourself feel all of that without trying to make it go away. Let yourself feel that tightness and that sensation that you're going to explode. See if you can let it be as strong as it wants to be.

JAMES: I'm going to blow up. I feel like I'm going to smash something.

THERAPIST: Great. You're doing it. Let those feelings be there. Even though it's pretty intense, you can just feel it. There is a lot of tightness in your body and that feeling like you're going to explode, and you can let yourself feel it. See if it's possible to say to yourself, "It's OK for me to feel this, even though it's intense."

JAMES: Yeah, but I just can't let him do this to me. I need to *do* something.

THERAPIST: OK. So you are having a thought that you can't let him do this to you. See if it's possible not to argue with that thought, but just to recognize that it's a thought and it might be true or it might not. Just notice that it's a thought and let it be there.

JAMES: But it *is* true. This guy is messing with me because he thinks he can get away with it.

THERAPIST: OK. (*Speaking slowly.*) There's a thought that it's really true, and that he's purposefully messing with you. When that thought is there, what do you notice in the body?

JAMES: It's the same. I feel hot everywhere and tense. I want to smash his face.

THERAPIST: OK. Let's stay with that. (*pause*) Just let yourself feel all of that without trying to change it. Feel those sensations in the body—that heat and tension. It's OK to feel it. It's OK that it's there. And you can feel that impulse to hit him. Just recognizing that you are strong enough to feel all of it and let it be there. You don't need to let it force you to act. Just feeling it all.

JAMES: OK. It's calming down a little.

THERAPIST: Sure. It might get stronger again or it might keep relaxing. Either way is fine. You are just being open to whatever comes up.

JAMES: Yeah. It's still relaxing. It's getting better.

THERAPIST: Good. Let's take some time and just stay with the feelings in your body. (*long pause*) What do you notice now?

JAMES: I'm a lot calmer.

THERAPIST: OK. Now as you are feeling calmer, picture that guy again from the dry cleaners. Let me know when he's there.

JAMES: Yeah, he's there. He never left.

THERAPIST: And what do you notice in your body now?

JAMES: I guess I feel sad, like a heaviness in my chest.

THERAPIST: Does it seem like he is trying to mess with you?

JAMES: No, but I just wish he cared more that this is going to screw up my whole day.

THERAPIST: OK, great. Tell him that.

JAMES: I wish you cared that this is going to screw up my day. (*Pauses and smiles.*) He said that he *does* care, but he doesn't know what to do. (*pause*) Wow. I feel a lot better.

This is an example of how mindfulness of the body and of thoughts can go together. You can see how I began with the body and shifted to his thinking when he was having strong thoughts. I went back and forth, depending on what was coming up for him. Let's go back through that session from the start.

He wanted to work on controlling his temper, so I asked for a recent example of his anger getting out of control. I find it's extremely helpful to look at specific situations rather than speaking in generalities, because everyone is different. When he told the story of his blowup at the dry cleaner's, he initially seemed defensive about his actions. He told the story as if he were reacting rationally to a horrible injustice, which is why I responded as I did. I reflected that he lost his temper and then explicitly asked if he would like to be able to react differently. Even though I had asked for an example of a time he wished he hadn't lost his temper, he didn't seem very regretful. I wanted to make sure we were really on the same team before moving forward, so I wanted an explicit agreement on our goals.

After a little thought, he agreed that he'd like to be able to stay calmer, but only if it didn't mean becoming a doormat. This was an important point of alliance that only arose because I noticed his ambivalence and commented. So we moved forward together with the goal of finding a way not to lose his temper, while also not becoming a doormat. I believe that he wouldn't have felt safe enough to fully engage with the exercise if he viewed me as potentially wanting to turn him into a passive victim.

Next, I had him picture himself back in that scene in order to get in touch with his anger. I knew the anger was present when he described the powerful tension in his body. Once it was there, I began with some basic mindfulness of the body instructions. His initial response sounded like he was having a hard time containing and accepting the intensity of his experience, so I affirmed his efforts and explicitly invited him to say, "It's OK for me to feel this, even though it's intense."

At that point, James responded with a thought, saying, "I just can't let him do this to me." The most important point here is that I recognized he was reporting a thought, and was not intimidated by it. I encouraged him to accept it, and offered some basic mindfulness of thinking instructions.

In moments like this, it can be tempting to want either to challenge the thought or agree with it. Although those techniques might be helpful in other situations, I believe that either one could have derailed things with James. Challenging the thought, in particular, would have likely triggered some profound defensiveness, and could have made him want to end the exercise. It would also miss an opportunity to help him practice a new way of relating to his thoughts. He knew how to argue with himself, but not how to observe his thoughts with spaciousness.

Although I didn't explicitly challenge his thought, James still responded defensively. When I suggested that his thought might or might not be true, he said, "But it *is* true." James was someone who identified with his thoughts in a powerful way. Especially when he was angry, he believed, "If I think it, then it's true." My goal was to give him an experience of relating to his thoughts differently, but it certainly wasn't easy. Again, I needed to remember that his responses were just thoughts and treat them accordingly with mindfulness of thinking instructions.

As I mentioned earlier, awareness of the body can help prevent us from being carried away by our thoughts. So I labeled each thought as a thought, and then asked about the sensations in his body. At this point, mindfulness of the body began to create some relief for James as he started to relate to his feelings with more open acceptance. You might notice how he described his feelings in the first person near the beginning of the exercise (e.g., "I feel like I'm going to explode"), and shifted into the third person at this point (e.g., "It's calming down a little"). I believe one of the reasons the practice started to click for James was that I had consistently responded to whatever he brought up with an open and accepting attitude. When he reported some amount of relaxation, I encouraged him to stay open to his experience, and he began to feel a lot calmer.

Then we revisited the original scene with more calmness and clarity. While calming down is valuable in itself, it can also lead to new insights. As he pictured the same man from the dry cleaner's, his anger turned into sadness. He just wished the man cared about his well-being.

After the exercise was over, this was an area we continued to explore. We talked about how he had assumed the man didn't care and even enjoyed causing him pain. We also talked about how he hadn't been aware that he had made this assumption, but had just reacted as though it were the truth. Because he has a Ph.D. and is academically oriented, I explained dual process theory, how System 1 automatically creates stories—even if we don't have enough information—and how mindfulness of thinking can help us notice that it's happening. He said that this explanation helped him not to feel ashamed about his habit of reacting on assumptions.

When he realized that he just wished the man cared more, I guided him to imagine actually saying that. I was betting on the likelihood that this visualization would help him recognize that the man actually did care more than James realized. However, it could have gone differently. James could have imagined the dry cleaning man saying something like, "It's just not my problem." If that had happened, we would have taken the opportunity to practice mindfulness with the sadness that would have come up. We would have spent some time grieving the reality that not everyone cares about our well-being as much as we wish they did. That also could have been a liberating experience, because he could have seen that he doesn't have to get so angry if he is willing to grieve when someone ignores his needs. However, the core lesson he got from this session was that his anger is often based on unquestioned assumptions. If he uses mindfulness of the body to calm his anger, he can get the clarity he needs to recognize those assumptions and question them.

BODY FIRST OR THOUGHTS FIRST?

With Susan, I began by asking about her thoughts, but with James, I began by having him connect with the feelings in his body. Is one better than the other?

The short answer is: Yes, start with the body. With almost all of my clients, I follow a pattern like I did with James. First, I get an explicit agreement about our goal. Second, I ask them to tell me about a recent example of their issue. Third, I ask them to imagine themselves in a scene that brings up the feelings associated with that issue. And fourth, I guide them to feel and accept those feelings as sensations in the body. It's only when the client's thinking interrupts this practice that I will shift to mindfulness of thoughts.

In Chapter 9, I cover some exceptions to this pattern for dealing with acute trauma, addiction, or psychosis.

MINDFULNESS OF THOUGHTS

1. Get an explicit agreement about therapeutic goal.
2. Ask client to recount a recent example of the issue.
3. Ask client to imagine being in a scene that brings up the feelings associated with that issue.
4. Guide client to feel and accept those feelings as sensations in the body.

Chapter 6

UNLOCKING A CLIENT'S NATURAL COMPASSION

"The teaching of the Buddha is very clear. If you do not love
yourself, you cannot love someone else and help him or her
suffer less. So the answer is clear: take care of yourself.
Nourish compassion, patience, freshness in you."
—Thich Nhat Hanh

There is a deep well of compassion inside every person. This chapter is about how we can tap into it. Once we know how to get in touch with the limitless source of compassion inside ourselves, the next few chapters will focus on how we can use that energy for transformation and healing.

As I mentioned earlier, Jaak Panksepp has discovered that one of the primary emotional circuits in the brain is about creating the experience of warmth, caring, and compassion. He calls it the Care Circuit, and it is essential for bonding and caretaking in all mammals, including humans. Evolutionary psychologists believe that compassion is so central to the human brain because our babies are so helpless (Nelson & Panksepp, 1998). In order to invest so much energy into the welfare of our children, we need to have a lot of motivation to care and love. As I write this, my son is 1 year old, and my whole life revolves around his needs.

The evolutionary drive to care for our children is normally very strong, but we know it can be weakened or even lost if circumstances are bad enough. On the other hand, scientists are now learning that the opposite is also true. Our capacity to care and love can be strengthened and applied to larger and larger circles through mental training (Neff & Germer, 2013; Davidson, 2012). It can also be used to regulate emotions, transform our suffering, and create deeper and more stable experiences of well-being.

The practices you will learn in this chapter will give you the ability to tap into this powerful source of compassion. You will learn how to engage the Care Circuit in the brain and strengthen it through deliberate practice. When you have developed this ability, it is like being able to flip a switch and turn the Care Circuit on whenever you need to. Again, once you have developed the ability to generate powerful feelings of compassion, the next few chapters explore how to direct that energy toward your suffering to create healing.

COMPASSION IN BUDDHIST PSYCHOLOGY

Before getting into specific practices, let's take a moment to explore how compassion is understood in Buddhist psychology. I believe that this background information will make the techniques easier to understand.

The word *karunā* is the Buddhist term (in both Pali and Sanskrit) that is generally translated as *compassion*. As I mentioned in Chapter 1, it is defined as the energy that heals suffering (Hanh, 2013a). Let me restate this for emphasis: *Compassion has the power to free others and ourselves from suffering.*

However, merely wanting to help someone is not enough. We also need to have enough understanding and skillfulness to know how to help effectively. Thich Nhat Hanh illustrates this idea by talking about a durian fruit. If you've never tried a durian, I can guarantee that it is like no other food you've ever tasted. To me, it tastes like a cross between lamb and vanilla ice cream, but I've heard it described in even stranger ways. In Vietnam, where Thich Nhat Hanh was born and raised, durian is a delicacy, but he says he doesn't like durian at all. He prefers pickled greens. However, he's had the experience many times of a student offering him a durian out of respect and standing there expectantly waiting for him to eat it. He says, "They are trying to bring me joy, but they are actually making me suffer."

We all have experiences like this in our own lives. We try to help someone and actually make things worse, or someone else does that to us. The important idea from this story is that just wanting to help isn't enough. We need to have enough understanding and skillfulness to help someone effectively.

This is why understanding (*paññā* in Pali, *prajñā* in Sanskrit) is almost always discussed alongside compassion. Compassion only becomes *true compassion*, with the ability to free us from suffering, when it is based in understanding—specifically, an understanding of the causes of our suffering. If we know what causes our suffering (not just the surface-level causes, but deep causes as well), then our compassion can lead to skillful action.

These two are often referred to as the "jewel in the lotus." The lotus is our compassion and the jewel is our clear understanding about the causes of suffering. Thich Nhat Hanh likes to say that mindfulness leads to insight and that insight leads to compassion. When we apply mindfulness to our suffering, our mind calms and we eventually come to understand its causes. This understanding gives rise to compassion.

THE FOUR-PART DEFINITION

Let's explore the meaning of compassion in more detail using a traditional Buddhist four-part definition. Those four parts are its nature, function, proximate cause, and manifestation. Although these might sound pretty technical, this kind of detailed analysis can lead to helpful insights about what compassion is and how to cultivate it.

- Part One: *The nature of compassion* is to want to remove suffering from oneself or another being. This means that, at its core, compassion is a type of wish or desire. You might have heard people say that Buddhism believes that desire is the cause of all suffering, but it's actually more complicated than that. The Dalai Lama himself often says that without the *desire* to liberate ourselves and others, we wouldn't be motivated to practice meditation at all.

- Part Two: *The function of compassion* is to inspire us to act. In other words, cultivating compassion—if it's done authentically—does not lead to passively accepting bad situations. It moves us to make things better.

- Part Three: *The proximate cause of compassion* is traditionally presented as the awareness that someone is suffering and wants to be happy. Understanding the proximate cause is important, because if you don't know what causes something, it's hard to generate more of it. The three key ingredients of compassion that I described in Chapter 1 can be understood as a way of elaborating on the proximate cause of compassion. Again, those ingredients are:

  1. We understand the person suffers.
  2. We understand the person wants to be happy and is attempting (however unskillfully) to create happiness for self and other.
  3. We understand that we are not fundamentally separate from each other.

  If we can apply this way of thinking to another person or to ourselves, it will reliably generate a feeling of compassion, and Jaak Panksepp has a theory about why. He believes that the Care Circuit evolved to get us to help someone (especially a child) who is in pain. When we see someone suffer, this brain circuit is activated in order to motivate us to help them (Panksepp & Biven, 2012).

- Part Four: *The manifestation of compassion* is described as a mind that is full of love and clarity. We know from research that developing compassion has powerfully positive effects on our physical and mental health. Scientists such as Barbara Fredrickson (1998) and Sonja Lyubomirsky (Nelson, Fuller, Choi, & Lyubomirsky, 2014) have documented how all positive emotions, and especially compassion, increase our ability to notice more possibilities, take another person's perspective, perform better on cognitive tasks, and even decrease the incidence of heart disease and cancer. When we know how to generate compassion from within, we begin to radiate more peace and stability, and we have an easier time getting along with others.

THE LIMITLESS VIRTUES

Let's look at one more way that compassion is explained in Buddhism before moving on to discuss techniques. The Four Brahmavihāras, also called the Four Limitless Virtues,[1] are a core teaching of every Buddhist school. These four virtues are loving-kindness (*mettā*), compassion (*karunā*), joy (*muditā*), and equanimity (*upekkhā*), and they are traditionally presented together because each quality is said to contain the other three (Hanh, 1996). Therefore, compassion (as we are defining it here) also contains loving-kindness, joy, and equanimity.

What does it mean to say that compassion *contains* these other qualities? I believe it is describing a specific way of relating to others and ourselves in which all four of these virtues come together. Beginning with ourselves, we recognize when we are suffering and that recognition inspires a deep desire to relieve that suffering. The desire to relieve our suffering (compassion) also comes with a desire to create happiness and well-being (loving-kindness). Extending out into wider and wider circles, we want ourselves and everyone else to be well and not to suffer. However, saying that we want people not to suffer is different from saying we are afraid of suffering. Our desire for wellness also contains a complete open acceptance toward any negative affect (equanimity). Imagine a friend is telling you about her suffering as you completely accept her as she is, while also wanting her to find happiness. We can feel radical acceptance of whatever arises in our experience, while also wanting ourselves to be well and free from suffering. Finally, when we recognize that well-being is present, we rejoice in that fact (joy). This is how the Four Brahmavihāras go together.

We might all agree that these four qualities are noble, but they certainly aren't easy to live by. How can we know if we are truly being compassionate, rather than just avoiding conflict? For example, if a coworker is regularly late for work and you always cover for her, is that action based in real compassion or could you be enabling her irresponsible behavior? It can be hard to know for sure. That is why the Brahmavihāras are often presented along with their *near enemies* to help us avoid mistaking a vice for a virtue. As you might remember from Chapter 1, a near enemy is a quality that is similar enough that you can mistake it for the real thing, but it's actually a type of opposite.

The near enemy of loving-kindness is a possessive type of love that wants to keep the beloved for oneself and has a strong attachment to them. Real loving-kindness, on the other hand, just wants the other person to be happy and involves no grasping or clinging.

The near enemy of compassion is pity, in which you see someone who is suffering and want to help, but at the same time you think you are better than that person. You might look down on the other person and think, "I want to help you because you are such a mess, and I'm a good person." That is really different than the kind of compassion where I can see myself in the other person and relate to them intimately.

The word *mudita* can be translated as *joy* or *sympathetic joy*. It specifically means rejoicing in the happiness of others. Its near enemy is being attached to positive emotions and trying to grasp onto them. In all of the transcripts in this book, whenever clients report feeling relaxed or happy, I encourage them to enjoy that feeling, but also to be open to anything else that might arise. That openness to whatever arises is what is meant by experiencing joy, but not being attached to it.

Upekkhā is hard to translate into English. Most people call it *equanimity*, but that word can have connotations of being aloof and detached, which is really different from what *upekkhā* means. Thich Nhat Hanh has started translating it as "inclusiveness" to stress the idea that it comes from being totally open to whatever comes up in our experience, rather than being defended or disconnected. The near enemy of equanimity/inclusiveness is indifference. Instead, we want to cultivate the equanimity that comes from being completely open, rather than from being closed or dissociated.

PRACTICING COMPASSION

Nearly all scientific research on the intentional development of compassion has used Buddhist meditation practices,[2] and most has focused on one specific technique that comes from a fifth-century meditation manual called the *Visuddhimagga* by a monk named Buddhaghosa.

First, I'll provide a quick overview of some other Buddhist techniques for cultivating compassion, and then I'll review this particular practice that has become so popular with researchers. Finally, we'll explore ways to apply compassion practices in a clinical setting.

Since cultivating compassion is such a core element of Buddhism, it makes sense that there are countless practices for doing so. Most Buddhist teachers consider living by an ethic of nonviolence to be essential in the development of compassion. As I mentioned earlier, mindfulness is also viewed as an indispensible practice because developing any virtue is easier with a serene and focused mind. There are certain ways of thinking that contribute to compassion, and these are cultivated with "analytical meditations." For example, the three key ingredients of compassion could be the basis for an analytical meditation if you were to spend some time intentionally focused on trying to see how they apply to your own life or your clients.

In the Tibetan tradition, one of the most important practices for cultivating compassion is called *tonglen*, which roughly translates to "sending and receiving." In this practice, we visualize taking the suffering of others into ourselves as we breathe in, and then radiating compassion to them as we breathe out. I have found this can be a wonderful practice for someone who has a basic level of mental stability, but I almost never use it with a clinical population.[3]

Now we will turn our attention to the form of compassion meditation that Richard Davidson (2012) has shown powerfully strengthens the happiness, optimism, and social attunement centers in the brain, and that Barbara Fredrickson (2013) has shown improves the quality of our relationships, our ability to cope with adversity, and even many measures of physical health. I'll first review how this practice is taught traditionally and then how it can be adapted for clinical situations.

This style of compassion meditation comes from the instructions for cultivating *mettā* in the *Visuddhimagga*,[4] which is why it is sometimes called *loving-kindness* meditation. We begin by recollecting the benefits of compassion and the dangers of hatred in order to generate a strong motivation to practice. This process of getting in touch with our motivation before beginning a specific practice is similar to connecting with the client's goals for therapy.

Once we have generated a strong motivation, we are instructed in Step 1 to begin sending love and compassion to ourselves. After we have accomplished this, Step 2 is to shift our love and compassion to a dear friend. Step 3 is to send compassion to a neutral person, Step 4 is sending compassion to someone who has harmed us, and Step 5 is sending compassion to all beings. Although this progression is a very popular practice in monasteries and retreat centers, there are a few reasons to believe it should be amended for working with a clinical population.

When Buddhaghosa explains why it makes sense to begin by sending compassion to oneself, he says that the self is the easiest possible object of compassion. However, that isn't always true. For many of us, and especially for our clients, sending compassion to ourselves is far from easy. For some clients, it would be the ultimate goal of therapy, rather than a simple place to begin. So instead of following his specific suggestion, I propose we follow Buddhaghosa's reasoning and begin with whatever image makes it easiest for the client to get in touch with the energies of warmth and compassion.

Here are a couple of instructions that can be helpful to use as a starting place. I will explain each of them and then provide three case examples.

1. *Explore different objects until you find one that brings up natural, uncomplicated feelings of warmth and love.* For some people this might be a baby, it might be an animal, or it might be a baby animal. We want to use whatever image helps turn on the Care Circuit and get the oxytocin and opiates flowing. We don't say, "Choose the person you love the most," since that is more likely to be a complicated relationship that brings up mixed feelings. We want something easy and uncomplicated. Pets and grandchildren are some of the most popular objects clients tend to choose for this exercise.

   It is important to have clients choose their own objects whenever possible, because there is no way for us to know what is going to be the most powerful image for someone else. I've had clients choose a cut flower, their childhood teddy bear, and even a rainstorm—none of which I could have guessed.

   Once clients have chosen an object for the exercise, we help them track the sensations in the body. If they report feelings of warmth and openness, it's going well. If not, we might consider either finding a new object or trying a different technique. I use this practice in all three examples below.

2. *Can you imagine a being—whether it's someone you've known, a religious figure, an image from nature, or even a fictional character—just someone who could completely love and accept you?* The first practice doesn't work for everyone. If a client can't find an image that inspires uncomplicated warmth and love,

then I will usually try these instructions. In this practice, the client might choose a grandmother, Jesus Christ, a white light, etc. Again, we are just looking for whatever imagery stimulates the Care Circuit, so the person/image can be living, dead, or even imaginary. What matters is that imagined object helps the client generate the feeling of being loved. I use this practice in the third example below.

Now we're ready to get into case examples. I start with a therapist from one of my workshops because it's relatively simple, and then explore more complicated situations with clients.

Example One: Beverly and Her Dog

Beverly was the clinical director of a large mental health agency in the Midwest. When she volunteered for this exercise, she said that she had chosen my training in part because she wanted to develop more compassion for herself. She was excited to learn new techniques and share them with her staff, but she also wanted to work on her own perfectionism.

BEVERLY: I'm extremely patient and nice to everyone that works for me, but I need to learn how to be nicer to myself.

THERAPIST: Great. Let's try this exercise and see how it goes. (*pause*) OK, so take a moment and explore different objects until you find one that brings up natural and uncomplicated feelings of warmth and love. (*pause*) Let me know when you've found something.

BEVERLY: (*Eyes closed.*) OK. I've got it.

THERAPIST: Good. What's your object?

BEVERLY: It's my dog.

THERAPIST: All right. (*pause*) So picture your dog there, and let the image be really clear, really vivid. (*pause*) And now let me know what sensations you notice in your body as you picture your dog. Is there tension, relaxation, warmth, or heaviness?

BEVERLY: I'm feeling a lot of warmth in my heart, like in my chest, and a sensation of opening in my throat and also my chest. (*pause*) My body is relaxed.

THERAPIST: Perfect. (*pause*) That's great. (*pause*) So just stay there with that image of your dog and deepen into that feeling of warmth and opening as much as you can. (*longer pause*) What's happening now?

BEVERLY: I'm feeling it. It's an open feeling and a lot of warmth in my chest and kind of my whole body.

THERAPIST: Great. (*pause*) So stay with that image of your dog and let it be really clear. I'm going to give you some phrases to experiment with. They might click for you or they might not. Please feel free to change them. (*pause*) So seeing your dog there, try saying to your dog, "May you be happy. (*pause*) May you be healthy. (*pause*) May you be safe. (*pause*) May you be loved." Let me know if those click for you.

BEVERLY: Yeah, they do.

THERAPIST: And what are the sensations in the body now?

BEVERLY: The warmth and opening are really strong and I feel pretty emotional.

THERAPIST: OK. Wonderful. Let's just stay with that for another minute or so. Really letting those feelings be strong. (*longer pause*) Now, let's see what happens if we try to include yourself in some of this compassion and love. We will try changing those phrases a little and see what happens. It might click and it might not, but that's OK. Picture your dog there, and try saying, "May we both be happy. (*pause*) May we both be healthy. (*pause*) May we both be safe. (*pause*) May we both be loved." Let me know what you are feeling in your body now.

BEVERLY: (*Eyes still closed*.) Kind of tense. When I focused on myself, it kind of made me nervous.

THERAPIST: OK. Let's go back to focusing on just your dog. Picture your dog there and let that image get really clear. (*pause*) Now come back to those phrases. [I repeat the original phrases a few times, and she reports that the warmth and relaxation return almost immediately. We spend a solid

5 minutes focused exclusively on her dog.] Now I'd like you to reflect for a moment on how your dog feels about you. What comes up?

BEVERLY: She loves me a lot.

THERAPIST: Great. As you picture her there and feel all of that warmth and love for her, also notice how much she loves you. What comes up for you now?

BEVERLY: Yeah. Even if it's hard for me to love myself, she loves me a lot. There's like a deeper relaxation I feel.

THERAPIST: Great. Stay with that. (*pause*) Now imagine your dog wishing for you to be happy and safe and loved. See if that's possible and let me know what comes up in your body.

BEVERLY: (*Eyes still closed.*) I almost want to cry. It feels really nice.

We stayed with that scene for a few more minutes, and then I asked if she could agree with her dog's wishes for her. Although that might sound a little strange, it was a way of bridging. She had expressed feeling comfortable being aware of her dog's affection for her, but tense when she imagined feeling affection toward herself. I was trying to see if we could build a bridge between those two different parts. She told me that she could agree with her dog's wishes, so we went back and tried directly sending compassion to herself again. For a second time, I offered her the phrases that said, "May we both . . . " and asked her to notice how she felt now. She reported that the statements made her feel deeply happy.

The main theme of this example is how to respond when the client encounters something challenging. We start with something as easy as possible and try to slowly expand from there. When we encounter something that feels difficult to the client, we immediately go back to what was easier.

This pattern comes from how the practice is taught traditionally. For example, if you were on a meditation retreat and learning this practice, you would begin by sending compassion to yourself. If that felt good, then you would move to a dear friend. If that also felt good, you would shift to a neutral person. You might feel really good until you arrive at the fourth step and imagine that person who has harmed you. When you picture him or her, you might feel no compassion at all, just tension. If that is the case, the instructions are very specific: You are instructed to go back immediately and *send yourself* more compassion. You don't try to argue yourself into thinking differently about that person or attempt to feign a feeling of compassion. You go back to what felt easy and natural. The teaching is that once you have received enough compassion for yourself, it becomes much easier to have compassion for others.

With Beverly, sending compassion to herself was the thing that was difficult, so we needed to adapt those instructions a little. She had felt really good sending love to her dog, so when she reported feeling tense at the thought of sending love to herself, we just went back to what was easier. We spent more time focused on her dog and let the feelings in her body get stronger. When the Care Circuit floods our body with oxytocin and opiates, loving anyone starts to feel easier.

I began this exercise by giving Beverly some meditation instructions and checked to see what sensations came up in her body. When she reported feeling warmth and openness, I knew she had understood the instructions and chosen an appropriate object. At that point, I knew that she had turned on her Care Circuit, so the next step would be turning it up to full strength.

I guided her to stay focused on the image of her dog and to try consciously letting herself deepen into those positive feelings. I added some phrases that are common to many forms of compassion practice to see if they might also help. Some clients respond well to these phrases and report that they really strengthen their positive feelings. Beverly was in that group. Other clients might respond to some phrases but not others, or want to change the wording. If a client likes three of them but not the fourth, then you can just drop the one he or she doesn't like. Any alternative phrases are OK as long as they are in harmony with the spirit of the Brahmavihāras. Some people prefer sending compassion by imagining an energy or light coming from their heart and not using phrases at all.

By the end of that exercise, we had learned that Beverly could now switch on her Care Circuit by concentrating on her dog, and turn up the strength by repeating those phrases. It was hard for her to direct love toward herself at first, but after spending more time focused on her dog, and then focused on her dog's love for her, it became possible. I suggested that she continue this practice everyday for at least 20 minutes. I explained that this practice could help transform her perfectionism, but she might benefit from adding another step later. The next step would be to imagine a time that she had made a mistake and send compassion to herself in that scene.

COMPASSION AS A TYPE OF WISH

The phrases that we use with compassion meditations are almost always expressed as a type of *wish*. We wish for happiness and freedom from suffering for ourselves and everyone else. We say, "May you be happy" or "May I be safe," etc. This way of expressing compassion comes from some of the earliest Buddhist discourses, and it is consistent in many different schools (Hanh, 1996).

Taken out of context, however, this wording can create a lot of confusion. We aren't wishing for safety or love out of some kind of deluded optimism. We don't believe it is actually possible for people to be safe or loved in every moment of their lives. We know that difficulties and disappointments are an inevitable part of life, and we certainly aren't trying to resist or deny that reality. In fact, there are many Buddhist practices that intentionally remind us that sickness, old age, death, and loss cannot be avoided. They are natural parts of life, and when we accept them without resistance, they don't hurt nearly as much.

An important key to understanding how compassion is viewed in Buddhism comes from putting these two kinds of practices together. We completely accept that illness and loss are inevitable, yet we still *wish* for everyone to be well and happy. But how does that make sense? A neuroscientist such as Jaak Panksepp (Panksepp & Biven, 2012) would say that we've evolved to have this powerful Care Circuit because we are so socially interconnected, and this part of our brain (when it is activated) causes us to wish that everyone could always be safe and loved.

A Buddhist would describe the same reality by saying that this deep wish is part of our "nature." In other words, we all wish that everyone could be safe and happy, but we live in a world in which that isn't going to happen. If we can learn to see the beauty of this situation—that every human being wishes we could all be happy, but lives in a world filled with problems—if that helps us to see how beautiful our human nature really is, then we understand the Buddhist perspective on compassion.

> *If we can learn to see the beauty of this situation—that every human being wishes we could all be happy, but lives in a world filled with problems—if that helps us to see how beautiful our human nature really is, then we understand the Buddhist perspective on compassion.*

Example Two: Patrick and His Niece

When Patrick was referred to me, he hadn't been able to work since his girlfriend broke up with him almost 2 weeks earlier, and he was in danger of losing his job. Patrick was a software designer in his late 20s who was suffering from severe anxiety and depression. He had grown up with an emotionally unstable mother who had attempted suicide twice while he was a child. She often had unpredictable outbursts of rage or uncontrollable crying. Patrick's father coped by being at home as little as possible, so Patrick and his siblings were left to deal with her by themselves. Patrick had always had difficulty regulating his emotions, and when his girlfriend left him, it was too much for him to bear.

In our first session, he told me about his family history and his recent breakup. Then, about halfway through that session, he expressed wanting to find something that could help him handle his intense feelings. He said, "I'm just too fragile. I need to be able to cope with things without collapsing."

THERAPIST: Sure. That's definitely something we can work on. We could pick that up later if you want to tell me more about what you've been going through, or we could start with that today. It's up to you.

PATRICK: I think I need some real help now. I'm struggling. I need something to get me through the week.

THERAPIST: Sure. Let me make sure I understand what you want. You are struggling right now with your emotions, and you want some way of coping better, whether that's being able to calm your feelings down or a way to tolerate them better. Is that right?

PATRICK: Yeah. (*Looks sad.*) Is that possible?

THERAPIST: It's definitely possible. I'm not sure if we'll find your answer today, but we can definitely start looking at different practices and see if we can find something.

PATRICK: Good. Let's do that.

THERAPIST: OK. Right now, on a scale from 0 to 10, where 0 is no distress at all and 10 is the worst you've ever felt, how bad is the distress you feel?

PATRICK: I don't know, like an 8 or 9.

THERAPIST: Thanks. And when is the last time you can remember it being a 4 or less?

PATRICK: Umm. Maybe when I was in college. I really don't remember.[5]

THERAPIST: OK. Thanks. So we'll try an exercise and see if it helps. You can never really tell what's going to click for someone, but we will try different things until we find something that works for you.

PATRICK: OK.

THERAPIST: So find a comfortable posture and with your eyes opened or closed, whatever is more comfortable for you, try exploring different objects until you find one that brings up natural and uncomplicated feelings of warmth and love. It might be a person, like a child, or an animal, and it could be anything. Let me know when you've got something.

PATRICK: (*Closes eyes.*) Yeah, I do. It's my niece.

THERAPIST: Great. So just picture her there and let the image be really clear. (*pause*) And now let me know what sensations come up in your body, like if there is any tension or relaxation, or if you feel any warmth.

PATRICK: Yeah. I feel a lot of love when I imagine her.

THERAPIST: Good. (*pause*) Great. (*pause*) When you are feeling that love, how does it show up in your body? Do you feel it in your chest, your throat, or somewhere else? Is it everywhere?

PATRICK: Yeah. I think it's everywhere, but mainly in my heart. I feel like . . . it's a good feeling. Maybe warm? Relaxed.

THERAPIST: OK. Perfect. Just let that warmth and relaxation be there. Stay with that image of your niece, and let these good feelings be there. (*longer pause*) Let me know what comes up or if it just gets stronger.

PATRICK: (*Starts to cry quietly.*) Yeah, it's still there. I just love her so much. She's such a pure, good person.[6]

THERAPIST: I know you do. (*pause*) As you are staying with this, is there anything difficult or uncomfortable coming up, or is it feeling like a relief?

PATRICK: It's a relief. It's like she is this one really beautiful thing, and if I keep thinking about her, life doesn't seem so bad.

THERAPIST: Good. That's wonderful. (*pause*) And now how much distress is there, from 0 to 10?

PATRICK: Umm. I feel good. It's maybe a 2. I feel a lot better.

For Patrick, picturing his niece was the key to turning on his Care Circuit and generating positive feelings. After just 15 minutes of this practice, he was feeling better than he could remember feeling for a long time. I review a session from later in his treatment in the next chapter, but for now I'll highlight a few key ideas from this session.

At the beginning of the session, I made sure that I understood Patrick's goals and got explicit confirmation that he wanted to begin working on them right away. Again, without this core element of alliance, our interventions won't be nearly as helpful.

Next, I took a quick assessment of his mood state. When he said his distress was an 8 or 9 out of 10, it corroborated what he said earlier about feeling overwhelmed by the intensity of his emotions. When someone is already overwhelmed, I'm more likely to use a compassion practice like this one rather than starting with mindfulness of the body. This kind of compassion practice can be understood as strengthening or resource building, and it seemed like an appropriate place to start. I was also really explicit that the first exercise we try might or might not work. I wanted to manage his expectations and avoid performance anxiety.

I gave him the same instructions I gave Beverly, and when he chose his niece, I checked in on the sensations in his body. Patrick reported feeling "love," so I affirmed that answer and then asked for more specific information about physical sensations in his body. He seemed a little unclear, but he gave me enough information that I could use it in two ways. First, I could be sure that the object was appropriate and his Care Circuit was on. Second, he used the words *warm* and *relaxed*, so I could use them in my instructions to help keep him focused on those feelings in his body.

When he began crying, I didn't know if some troubling thoughts were coming up, or if he was just experiencing a lot of relief. He might have been thinking, "Why didn't anyone ever love me as much as I love her?" or "Why am I not more involved in her life?" Distressing thoughts can definitely come up in exercises like this. On the other hand, I know that some clients experience such a huge relief from their oppressive negative emotions during self-compassion exercises that they start crying tears of happiness. I asked him explicitly which was happening so I would know if he needed extra guidance. If he were having a negative reaction, I could have tried mindfulness of thinking instructions or just switched to a different style of compassion meditation.

At the end of the session, I told Patrick that the more time he spends practicing this technique over the next week, the better he would feel. I said, "Twenty minutes a day is good, 2 hours is better, and all day long would be ideal."

Example Three: Maria and Jesus on the Cross

Maria was referred to me because she hadn't been making progress with her previous therapist. She was severely depressed, hoarding, and had begun to stop taking basic care of herself. She relied on her adult daughter for almost everything, and often wouldn't eat unless her daughter brought food to her house. Her daughter also drove her back and forth to therapy.

Maria was a petite woman in her late 50s, and although she was not financially poor, her appearance was usually disheveled. Her previous therapist told me she had been neglected and emotionally abused as a child.

The following transcript is from the middle of our first session. I had already done some assessment and decided that she did not seem to be a risk to herself as long as her daughter continued caring for her. I had spoken with her daughter, who was much more concerned with her mother's well-being than her own stress, so that situation seemed safe.

> THERAPIST: What I'd really like to know is how I might be able to help you. What kinds of changes would you like to see in your life?
>
> MARIA: (*Looking down.*) I don't know.
>
> THERAPIST: Sure. That makes sense. (*Pause, then speaking slowly.*) I'm just here because I want to help if I can. I can't say that I'll definitely be able to help you make things better in your life, but I think that I might, if that's what you want. I've helped a lot of people in similar situations to yours. (*She looks up and makes eye contact with a smile; seems hopeful but afraid.*) I want to understand what you really want from therapy. We can spend time just talking. You can ask me anything you want or tell me about yourself. (*pause*) If you decide you want to have more energy or feel better, we could try to do that.
>
> MARIA: What do you think would help me?
>
> THERAPIST: I have a couple of ideas we could try. I think it

would be about trying to help you have a little more energy and feel a little better. Would you want to try that?

MARIA: Sure.

THERAPIST: [Because Maria answered making good eye contact and without any hesitance in her voice, I feel confident we have an alliance on goals.] OK. So we'll try a couple different things and hopefully something will help. If something doesn't feel right, just let me know and we will switch to a different practice.

MARIA: OK.

THERAPIST: So let's start by seeing if you can picture some object that brings up natural and uncomplicated feelings of warmth and love. It might be a baby or an animal or anything else. Just something you can picture that brings up natural and uncomplicated warmth and love.

MARIA: (*Closes eyes for a minute and then opens them.*) I don't think so.

THERAPIST: Sure. (*pause*) Can you tell me about what came up when you tried?

MARIA: Anything I pictured just made me feel bad, like my daughter or my grandkids. I'm just no good for anybody. (*Looking down.*)

THERAPIST: Thanks. You did that perfectly (*she raises an eyebrow*), and it seems like it's not the right practice for you. Like I said, these different practices don't work for everybody, so we often have to try a few before we find something that's a good fit.

MARIA: OK.

THERAPIST: Now, let's try something different. Again, this might work for you or it might not, but we are just trying different things until we find one that helps. So let's see if you can picture someone who could completely love and accept you. It might be someone you've known, or a religious figure, an image from nature like a white light, or even a fictional character. Just see if you could picture someone who could really love and accept you.

MARIA: (*Closes eyes again and smiles.*) Yes. I picture Jesus on the cross.

THERAPIST: Great. That's perfect. Now just let that image get really clear. (*pause*) You're picturing Jesus on the cross and knowing how He loves and accepts you. (*pause*) Let me know what you are feeling. Do you notice any sensations in your body, like warmth or tension, heaviness, anything like that?

MARIA: My body feels light. (*Eyes still closed as she nods her head.*) Maybe some love in my heart.

THERAPIST: Perfect. Let's just stay here. Keep picturing Jesus there and knowing how He loves and accepts you. See if you can really let yourself feel light and feel that love in your heart.

MARIA: Yeah, I feel it. (*Mood seems somewhat improved, but tone of voice is flat. I sense some ambivalence.*)

THERAPIST: Great. Now we are going to experiment with some phrases. They might fit or they might not. You can change them or just forget them. (*pause*) So, picturing Jesus there and he says to you, "May you be happy." (*pause*) "May you be healthy." (*pause*) "May you be safe." (*pause*) "May you be loved." Let me know what comes up, or what you notice in your body.

MARIA: I don't deserve it. (*Eyes still closed; face looks tense and she shakes her head a little.*)

THERAPIST: OK. Thanks. (*pause*) Keep staying there with Jesus on the cross. (*pause*) Now I'd like you to try saying, "Even though I don't deserve it, I see how much He loves me."

MARIA: (*Quiet for a moment and then starts crying.*) It's true.

THERAPIST: (*Longer pause while she continues crying.*) What are you thinking or feeling now? Does this make you feel bad or good?

MARIA: (*Still crying.*) It's good. (*Pause until her crying calms down.*) He loves me no matter what.

THERAPIST: That's wonderful. Can you tell me how you feel in your body now? Any tension or warmth?

MARIA: I feel so good right now. Thank you.

We spent the next 10 or 15 minutes just giving her the space to connect with that good feeling. She continued to report feeling more and more relaxed, and her mood continued to improve over that whole time. Near the end of the session, I told her that she could use this practice as a way to allow Jesus's love to heal her. I suggested that she picture Jesus every morning and every evening and say to herself, "Even though I don't deserve it, I see how much He loves me." I let her know that she might want to change those words over time, and that is fine. We will continue with this case in Chapter 8.

Going back to the beginning of this transcript, you can see that I was trying to create an alliance around goals. Many therapists prefer not to move into the treatment phase in a first session, especially with a shy client like Maria. They would just want to build rapport and give her lots of space to open up. I think that can be great, but my personal style is to make sure my clients understand that we *can* begin working on relieving their suffering at any time. Many of my clients will say they just want us to get to know each other for a few sessions, but others are happy to start working right away.

In this case, Maria said she wanted to see if we could find something that might help her feel better. I chose to begin with a self-compassion meditation because she presented like someone with very low affect tolerance, and I thought she could use some resource building. However, the first set of instructions we tried didn't work for her at all. There are a couple points I want to make about this initial failed attempt.

First, I had prefaced the exercise by saying it would be OK if it didn't work for her. I believe that Maria would have been much more upset by the experience if I hadn't said that. Second, after Maria told me it hadn't worked, I asked her to give me some details about what came up for her when she tried. Although I'm aware that my question could have brought up some shame for her, I believe that this information is just too important to ignore. If she had said, "I tried to picture a baby but I couldn't," then I would have known the issue was about her ability to visualize.

Instead, it was clear that her powerful self-criticism was getting in the way of being able to feel warmth and love for the people in her life. Rather than sticking with this practice, I thought it might be better to try something different. I gave her the second set of instructions, and I could tell by her smile and tone of voice that it was working for her. We had succeeded in finding a way to turn on her Care Circuit. However, turning up the strength would prove more difficult.

When I gave her the standard phrases, she had a negative reaction. So I needed to make sense out of what was going on for her. She could experience Jesus's love, but if she imagined him explicitly wishing her well, it brought up the idea that she didn't deserve it. I paused in that moment and put myself in her shoes. I imagined being able to feel Jesus's love when he was not speaking, and then feeling bad and undeserving when he explicitly wished me well. I explored that in myself for a moment and noticed a few things. First, I felt more vulnerable when he was specifically focused on me, and safer when he wasn't. Second, I had a felt sense that the core belief, "I don't deserve love," was not going to shift very easily. As I was trying to put myself in her shoes, I said to myself, "I know He loves me, and I don't deserve it," as a way of trying to see how those two ideas could fit together. When I said it, I felt emotionally moved, so I thought to ask her to try. She did, and it had the same effect. Incorporating that core belief into the exercise actually made it much more powerful. In Chapter 8 we explore how therapy progressed with Maria and how we used the energy of compassion to heal her self-criticism.

UNLOCKING COMPASSION

Basic Instructions
- "Explore different objects until you find one that brings up natural, uncomplicated feelings of warmth and love."
- "Can you imagine a being—whether it's someone you've known, a religious figure, an image from nature, or even a fictional character—someone who could completely love and accept you?"

Core Concepts
- Start with whatever is easiest and expand from there.
- If the client has any difficulty sending compassion to a particular object, let it go and return to an object that was easier.
- If the client says something you don't understand, put yourself in his or her shoes and see if you can relate to it.

Chapter 7

USING COMPASSION TO HEAL AND TRANSFORM SUFFERING IN THE PAST AND PRESENT

Now that we understand how to tap into the deep well of compassion that exists in each of us, our next task is to use that energy to heal and transform suffering. The simplest way to explain how this process works is to go back to the analogy of applying salve to a wound. When we are able to send compassion directly to our suffering—when it makes direct contact—the result is healing. The compassion can come from oneself or from another person; either way is fine. What matters most is that the *part of oneself that is suffering* is embraced with open acceptance and love.

Thich Nhat Hanh (2011) uses the image of a mother embracing her crying baby to illustrate how this process works. When the baby starts to cry, the mother responds by picking him up and holding him with her full compassionate presence. If the mother is calm, peaceful, and loving, the baby begins to feel better right away. Our own suffering is just like that. If we can hold our suffering like a mother holds her crying baby, with that kind of openness and warmth, this can be enough to create real transformation and healing.

However, sometimes being held is not enough. If a baby is hungry, wet, or in pain, true compassion requires that the mother address the source of the problem. She holds the baby with compassion and that helps him feel somewhat calmer, but if the baby is still crying, the mother begins to inquire into the causes of his suffering. Once she understands the causes, it is only natural for her to act to remedy them. You wouldn't expect a mother to notice her baby has a wet diaper and then just empathize without changing it. That would be weird. When she understands what is causing the baby's suffering, the mother takes action. The practice of self-compassion is the same.

We are instructed to recognize when suffering is present in us and to hold it just like a mother holds her crying baby: with that kind of openness and warmth. Often that's all we need to feel better, but sometimes it's not. Sometimes there are deeper problems we need to understand and address. We recognize that we're suffering, and we hold that suffering with compassion until the mind begins to feel a little calmer. We might practice feeling our suffering as sensations in the body, or use some kind of visualization. (More specifics are considered in the examples that follow.) As the mind settles down, we have more clarity with which to inquire into the causes of our suffering. Is there some painful experience from our past that is being triggered, or some negative core belief that's causing us to suffer? Whatever it is, we can respond skillfully once we understand.

HOW THE MIND CONSTRUCTS EXPERIENCE

How can we direct compassion right at the source of our suffering? In order to answer that question, we need to have a basic model of the mind and mental functioning.

There are countless theories from cognitive science, Western psychology, Buddhist psychology, and neuroscience about how the mind constructs experience. Although there are major disagreements among different theorists, there are also a few important points of general consensus. I'll attempt to present a view that is simple enough that most major contemporary theorists could accept it. Then we'll explore how this model can inform our practice of self-compassion.

1. *The past informs the present*: This concept should make sense to everyone. Our present experience is colored by our past experiences. In a given situation, my emotional reaction might be primarily caused by a present circumstance (e.g., appropriate grieving when a friend dies), or it might be primarily caused by a past experience (e.g., my mother was emotionally distant, and I tend to feel rejected for very small reasons). Every emotional response is caused by a mix of past and present factors, but often one is dominant over the other.

2. *Constructivism*: As I mentioned earlier, our automatic System 1 thinking always creates stories to make sense out of our experience. This is the process of constructing meaning, and it generally occurs outside of our conscious awareness. These stories and meanings actually have a bigger impact on us than what objectively happens in our lives. For example, if someone wins a sum of money but interprets it in a negative way (e.g., it means that something bad will happen soon, because nothing good can happen without something bad happening too), that good luck could make the person anxious instead of happy. Our stories can be concretized into *core beliefs* about who we are and the kind of world in which we live. These core beliefs have a huge impact on the amount of suffering and happiness in our lives.

3. *Modularity or psychological "parts"*[1]: Many people believe we can only have one thought or feeling at a time, but that is just not true. Looking at our basic neuroanatomy, we know that the brain is a parallel distributed processor (Rumelhart, McClelland, & PDP Research Group, 1995), which means it has many different processes[2] happening in any given moment, including multiple neural networks in the emotion and cognition centers of the brain firing at the same time.

   All of these processes usually function as a harmonious,

well-integrated whole,[3] but sometimes there are problems. For example, the experience of ambivalence can be understood as having different "parts" of oneself in conflict about a given situation. Maybe there's a part of me that wants to exercise more and another part that dreads exercise. Maybe there is a part of me that hates my father and another part that desperately wants his approval. Either way, we can see that an awareness of modularity, or psychological parts, is vital for understanding how we think, feel, and act. This will be even more apparent in clinical examples below.

Again, these parts are largely invisible when they are functioning harmoniously. We only become aware of them when there is conflict.

Many neuroscientists use the term *integration* to describe optimal mental health (Siegel, 2001). When all of our different parts and processes are well integrated, we function optimally. Psychological problems arise when these parts are poorly integrated. The concept of integration only makes sense in the context of modularity.

I believe that understanding modularity is extremely important for psychotherapy, and I will explain why in more detail in the next chapter. Although there are some psychological theories that attempt to name a certain number of "parts" or to assign them certain roles, it is important to understand that this kind of categorization is not an essential feature of modularity. We know that psychological parts exist; however, there is not a certain number (there are many), and the roles they play are idiosyncratic and fluid.

Any system of categorizing psychological parts (e.g., internal family systems) can be compared to a system for categorizing people (e.g., scapegoat, peacemaker). It can offer helpful insights in certain circumstances, but it will also tend to ignore important individual factors that don't fit the model.[4]

Basic learning theory tells us that different psychological parts will have access to different information, which is why they can come to different conclusions about a given situation. The part of me that hates my father might have developed when I was a teenager. It is aware that the way he treated me was wrong and has no empathy for him. The part that wants his approval was more likely formed when I was very young, and blames myself whenever he gets angry. There might be another part of me that was formed as an adult and sees how overwhelmed he was when I was young and how badly his parents had treated him, so that part grieves the emotional abuse I experienced but also feels bad for him. If I come to you for therapy, it is likely that these different parts will be poorly integrated at first. They aren't sharing enough information and might not be communicating at all. They each have different emotional responses to situations in my life, which leads to feelings, thoughts, and behaviors that don't make sense to me. Each part is likely suffering and in need of compassion, even if I'm not consciously aware of their existence.

To review, the concept of modularity refers to the different psychological parts we all possess. We are aware of some, yet many are implicit until they are discovered in therapy (or meditation). They usually function harmoniously, but they can also have conflicts, be formed at different times, be aware of different information, and prioritize different needs. We can learn to help them communicate and resolve their conflicts to create greater integration and mental health (see case examples in this chapter).

Finally, self-sabotage can be considered a special form of ambivalence. Lots of people undermine their own goals in therapy and in life. They either do things or fail to do things that they know will prevent them from achieving their goals. Harvard psychologist Robert Kegan describes this kind of ambivalence as having "competing commitments" (Kegan & Lahey, 2001). We can also just call it *self-sabotage*. For example, I might come into therapy saying I'm painfully shy and want to gain more confidence. Then a few sessions into our work together, you help me discover that my mother was shy and my father was brash and arrogant. I decided when I was very young never to be like my father. On the one hand, I have a conscious commitment to develop some confidence; that part of me knows it would be a good thing. However, *there is another part* that was formed when I was young and feels completely differently about developing confidence. It is operating from a core belief that says, "You can either be like Mom or like Dad. So don't be like Dad." That part has been fighting my attempts to gain confidence without my realizing it. Bringing compassion to competing commitments is an important skill, which we'll explore in the case examples.

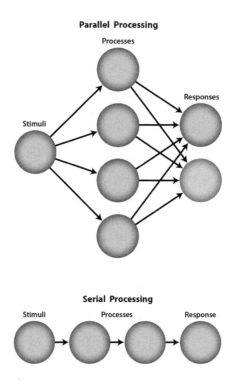

How does this model of the mind relate to practicing self-compassion? If we want to direct compassion right at the source of our suffering, there are a few different targets we can keep in mind. Sometimes the most powerful place to send compassion is to myself in the present as I'm going through a difficult circumstance. Other times it can be more powerful to picture myself in the past, like when I was a child, and direct compassion there. If my suffering is primarily coming from a negative core belief, I can send compassion to the part of myself that holds that belief. If there is a part of me that is criticizing myself or sabotaging my goals, I should try to understand that part and send compassion to it. I will illustrate sending compassion to the present and past in this chapter, and then look at core beliefs and self-sabotage in the next.

WHERE TO DIRECT COMPASSION

Toward . . .

- The present
- The past
- A negative core belief
- The inner critic or other self-sabotaging part

Example One: Self-Compassion in the Present

Megan was the executive vice president of sales at a medical software company. She came to see me for help dealing with stress. She said that her job was harming her marriage, and she wanted to learn how to cope differently. In our first session, we mainly focused on building an alliance. She used the time to reflect on how she handles stress from work, as well as her fears that she will have to sacrifice career success to avoid losing her marriage.

The one intervention I made during this session was pointing out that she seemed to assume that the only way to perform at work was to maintain this intense level of stress. I said that could be true, but we might be able to find a way for her to work just as effectively without experiencing so much stress.

In our next session, we jumped right into trying to understand her work stress. I asked her to tell me about the most stressful things at her job, and she said it's mostly when she has to collaborate with people from the tech support department in her company. She isn't their supervisor, and she has lost several clients because of how slow they were to respond to her needs.

MEGAN: I've learned that I just have to keep calling and nagging and even sometimes yelling at them or they won't respond to me at all.

THERAPIST: And that's the most stressful thing for you?

MEGAN: Absolutely, because if I can't get them to *do their jobs* (*sarcastic tone*), then I can lose clients, and it's my job to bring in clients.

THERAPIST: Sure. So what is it about possibly losing a client that makes it so stressful? Is it losing the income or something else?

MEGAN: Well, I don't know. It's not like I'm hard up for money. I think that I really work hard to do an excellent job and I don't want anyone taking that away from me.

THERAPIST: Sure. So is that the most stressful part—the possibility of not excelling, or is it feeling out of control, or something else?

MEGAN: This is good. Umm. I think that when I meet an obstacle to succeeding, I just need to push through it, but these guys don't work for me, so it's really frustrating.

THERAPIST: OK. I think I'm getting it. Let me know if this sounds right. You really want to do an excellent job and overcome whatever obstacles are in your path. When you don't have the power to fix a problem, it's just incredibly frustrating. Is that right?

MEGAN: Yeah, and it eats me up inside. I can't let it go and I obsess over it. I find myself getting so mad at those guys.

THERAPIST: OK. So let me see if I understand what you want today. You'd like to see if it's possible not to feel so upset and stressed out by these problems at work. Is that right?

MEGAN: I'd like them not to happen.

THERAPIST: OK. You want to see if it's possible for you to handle these problems differently so they are easier to resolve. Is that right?

MEGAN: Yeah. That sounds good.

THERAPIST: OK. Can you walk me through a recent time this happened? It would be a time when you were feeling really powerless to get the support you needed from the tech people and how you were responding didn't seem to make things better.

MEGAN: Sure. (*pause*) OK. So, a new client calls me and says he has a problem and hasn't heard back from the tech department, so I make the call myself. The guy I spoke with . . . I'm getting stressed out just telling you about it. He says they are handling it and just wants to get off the phone, so I'm like, "No, you aren't, and that's why I have to call you! (*angry tone*) This client needs to get an email immediately acknowledging you're working on it, and it needs to be fixed by the end of the day!"

THERAPIST: Great. Pause right there. (*Speaking slowly.*) You are on the phone with that tech person. He wants to get off the phone, and you are telling him what you need. Pause right there. (*pause*) Now tell me what sensations you notice in your body. Is there tension, relaxation, heaviness, lightness?

MEGAN: (*Closes her eyes.*) Yeah. My whole body is tense, especially my jaw and my face. And my heart is racing.

THERAPIST: Great. (*pause*) Perfect. Let's see if it's possible just to stay there for a minute or so. See if you can allow yourself to feel that tension and that racing heart; just let it be there without trying to change it at all. Just let yourself feel it all.

MEGAN: (*Eyes still closed.*) I can feel it. (*pause*) I want to yell at him, "You need to do your job!"

THERAPIST: Good. Stay right there. Stay with that tension and the racing heart. Let those feelings be there. And there is this thought: You want him to do his job. Feel all of that. (*pause*) Now try saying to yourself, "This person might not help my client like I want him to, and I might not be able to change that." Let me know what comes up when you say that.

MEGAN: Ugg. (*Furrows her brow; eyes still closed.*) I want to change it. I just want him to do his job!

THERAPIST: Perfect. Let that thought be there too. You want him to do his job so badly, and you know you might not be able to make that happen. All the tension and other feelings are there, and you are just letting it all be there.

MEGAN: OK. It's hard. (*long pause*)

THERAPIST: Now try saying to yourself, "I really want to do a great job, but this other person isn't helping me. This is hard, but I'm doing everything I know how to do." (*pause*) See if you can say that to yourself and have some compassion for yourself in this difficult circumstance. Maybe even say, "Megan, I know you want to fix this problem, but sometimes other people don't help you. You are doing everything you can and I love you."

MEGAN: Say that to myself? OK. (*Long pause as she repeats the sentence silently, then her face softens dramatically.*) Let me say that again: "Megan, you are doing everything you can and I love you." (*Starts to cry and her face looks very relaxed.*)

THERAPIST: (*pause*) Yeah. That's perfect. Let's just stay there. Keep practicing with that sentence and change it if you want.

I guided Megan to stay with this practice for as long as it was feeling powerful for her. She was quiet for about 10 minutes, and every minute or so I would repeat her sentence out loud to make sure her mind hadn't drifted too far. Then we processed her feelings a little, and she told me how much relief she felt when she sent love and compassion to herself in that frustrating moment. She said it was like magic.

In the second half of that session, I had her imagine going back and calling that tech support person again. Her frustration returned, but she immediately used self-compassion to calm and soothe herself. When I asked what she wanted to say to him from this more peaceful and grounded place, she laughed out loud. She said, "I can't believe I thought yelling at this person was going to do any good. I would offer to help him and say I can talk to his supervisor about taking other things off his plate. I would treat him like a person. I can't believe how silly I was being! That's just not how to motivate this kind of guy."

Returning to the transcript, the first part of this session was focused on the principle of *accurate empathy* that I mentioned in Chapter 3. When Megan described how slow response times had led to her losing clients, I believe many therapists would have said something like, "Yes, that sounds frustrating." However, I kept asking her why it was frustrating. At that point in the session, I was trying to put myself in her shoes, which helped me realize that it would be entirely possible for someone to view this situation as an inevitable part of working on a team rather than something so stressful it would impact her marriage. I knew there needed to be some other factor involved that was contributing to her stress.

She eventually articulated that she couldn't stand being unable to fix a problem, which made me wonder about whether she might have a pretty low frustration tolerance, at least in that part of her life. As usual, I asked her to get in touch with her symptom by imaging herself back in a situation where it was triggered. We slowed down her process, explored the feelings in her body with mindfulness, and recognized some of the strong thoughts that came up.

In this example, I didn't just reflect her thoughts and feelings back to her. I also explicitly emphasized the fact that she might not be able to get the tech person to do what she wants him to do. There are some problems in life that we can fix and others that we can't. That is just a part of being human. I could see that Megan was not comfortable with this existential truth, and her inability to "accept the things we cannot change," to quote the Serenity Prayer, was a major source of her stress. Therefore, I wanted to try to focus on finding a way for her to feel at peace in the face of a problem she might not be able to solve.

So there she was: confronted with a problem, reminded that she might not be able to fix it, and guided to observe her thoughts and bodily sensations with open acceptance. In this example, I chose to introduce self-compassion rather than continuing with mindfulness instructions because that is the practice that occurred to me when I imagined putting myself in her shoes. I don't have an algorithm to compute when to use one type of practice over another, and I wouldn't trust one if someone created it.

I believe this skill always begins with trial and error and eventually becomes more and more informed by the clinician's own personal experience with these practices. That is why I focus on helping therapists develop their own personal self-compassion practice as a major component of clinical training.

Finally, you might have noticed my self-compassion instructions were pretty informal, especially compared to the previous chapter. I imagined myself in her position—feeling gut-wrenching frustration at being unable to fix a problem—and once I felt like I could really connect with that experience, I asked myself how I would practice with it. My years of meditation told me that I needed self-compassion, so I asked myself how I could express that feeling in a way that would make a real impact. The words, "You're doing your best and I love you," came up pretty immediately, so I adapted that sentiment into some instructions for Megan. If those instructions had fallen flat, I might have tried to use a more traditional form.

Example Two: Continuing with Patrick and Compassion for the Past

Is it truly possible to heal the past? We have all suffered, and we all carry pain from our past into our present relationships and decisions. Many of our clients are so impacted by past events that living in the present and appreciating what is good or beautiful in this moment can seem impossible. So we might ask, to what extent can this situation be changed? We certainly can't erase the past or change things that objectively happened, so are we doomed to have our lives dictated by them?

Buddhism and neuroscience are both very clear in saying that it's possible to free ourselves from past suffering so it no longer limits or obstructs our ability to be happy in the present. This is possible because, as Thich Nhat Hanh often says, the past is contained in the present. If we imagine a 100-year-old tree, we can see that the 50-year-old tree is contained within it. You could count the rings and point to the exact place where the 50-year-old tree is present in the 100-year-old tree. We can see that the 20-year-old tree and the 10-year-old tree are all concretely present in the 100-year-old tree.

It is the same with us. Every experience we have is recorded in the shapes of connections in the neural networks in our brains. If a past experience is still impacting us in any way, that is because the connections that were made during that experience are still concretely present in our brains. Someday our brain imaging technology could be accurate enough that we could point to the exact place that our brain stores the experience of our 5-year-old self being humiliated by an older sibling, or our 10-year-old self being bitten by a neighborhood dog.

We cannot change what happened in the past, but we can change how it impacts us. The metaphor of the rings in a tree shows us how the past can be accessed in the present because its mark remains within us. Through the process of reconsolidation that we discussed in Chapter 2, we know that it's possible to activate the neural network where a past experience or core belief is stored and transform it using self-compassion.

With this in mind, let's return to Patrick from the previous chapter. In our last session, he had learned to activate his Care Circuit by picturing his niece. The next week, Patrick came in and said he had practiced that technique for at least 30 minutes every day. He said that he had been able to go to work 3 out of 5 days, and been relatively productive working from home on the other 2 days. He was extremely thankful for this new practice and said that 30 minutes in the morning improved his mood so much that he could function for most of the day.

For the next four or five sessions, I mostly coached him on using this new practice to build resilience and cope with adversity. We learned that practicing for 30 minutes in the morning and 30 before bed made a huge difference in his day-to-day functioning.

Patrick also learned that he could pause and picture his niece for three breaths whenever he started feeling stressed or sad. By this time, he was back to excelling at work and felt ready to go deeper with therapy. He told me that despite all of the energy he got from picturing his niece, he still felt bad about himself a lot of the time.

PATRICK: I'm doing so much better, but if I'm honest, I still don't really like myself. It's like I feel embarrassed all the time or like people are going to realize I'm a phony.

THERAPIST: OK. (*pause*) Let me see if I'm understanding. Even though your mood and energy have been a lot better, there is still this sense of not liking yourself or feeling embarrassed. Is that right?

PATRICK: Yeah. Is that something we can work on? Can that change?

THERAPIST: Absolutely. I've worked with a lot of people who have been able to change those kinds of feelings. I can't say how long it will take, but we can definitely start today. We can look at some different practices and see if any of them seem like they could help you.

PATRICK: Great. Let's do that.

THERAPIST: Sure. Before we start, what is the level of distress you are feeling right now, where 0 is feeling fine and 10 is the worst you've ever felt?

PATRICK: I guess I'm at like a 4 or 5.

THERAPIST: OK, thanks. (*pause*) Let's start with the practice of picturing your niece. With your eyes opened or closed, get a clear image of her, and let me know when she's there.

PATRICK: (*Closes eyes.*) She's there.

THERAPIST: And what are the feelings in the body now?

PATRICK: A lot of warmth in my heart, and I feel open and relaxed.

THERAPIST: Great. Let's just stay here, and really let yourself deepen into this experience. (*long pause*) Now, how old is your niece as you're picturing her?

PATRICK: She's 5 or 6.

THERAPIST: Great. (*pause*) Can you picture yourself as a 5- or

6-year-old boy standing next to her? Let me know if you can picture that.

PATRICK: Sure.

THERAPIST: What do you notice in your body now?

PATRICK: (*Eyes still closed.*) I just get angry. I hate that little jerk.

THERAPIST: OK. (*Speaking slowly.*) Can you tell me what you don't like about him?

PATRICK: He's just this worthless little whiney baby who cries all the time.

THERAPIST: OK. Now, let's see what happens if you go back to just picturing your niece. She's there by herself again. Let me know what comes up when she's there by herself.

PATRICK: Yeah. I relax a lot. (*big sigh and long pause*) The love comes back when I picture her.

THERAPIST: OK, great. Let's stay here for a minute or so. (*long pause*) Now I'd like you to picture another little 5-year-old boy next to your niece. This boy is *not* you, but he looks a little like you. He's also lived through a lot of the same things you'd lived through at his age. His mom is really unstable and his dad is never home. (*pause*) Can you picture that boy next to your niece?

PATRICK: Yeah, I can.

THERAPIST: Can you describe him a little? Does he look sad or happy or some other way?

PATRICK: He looks really sad. (*pause*) My niece is trying to cheer him up. She just gave him a toy. (*Looks very emotional, like he might cry.*)

THERAPIST: Perfect. Let's stay there for a moment. (*pause*) Now let me know how you feel about this little boy or what you might want to say to him.

PATRICK: I just feel sad for him.

THERAPIST: Is there anything you'd want to say to him?

PATRICK: "I'm sorry you're so sad." (*pause*) "I wish you had a better life."

THERAPIST: When you picture him, could you feel the same kind of love you feel for your niece? Picturing them together, can you feel that love and warmth for both of them? You might try saying, "May you both be happy and safe."

PATRICK: (*a lot of emotion in his voice*) Yes. I can feel that.

THERAPIST: Wonderful. (*pause*) Now see what comes up if you try saying to him, "No matter how your parents treat you, you are still lovable. It is not your fault."

PATRICK: (*Crying a little.*) Yes. I think that's true.

THERAPIST: (*long pause*) Now, I'd like you to imagine yourself as a 5-year-old boy standing next to these two other kids. Your niece is there, the other boy is there, and you are there as a 5-year-old. Let me know when you can picture that.

PATRICK: Sure.

THERAPIST: Good. Notice how those two boys both look pretty sad. They have lived through a lot of the same things, and they are both sad. See if you can recognize that they are also both lovable.

PATRICK: (*pause*) Yeah, I can see that. They didn't ask for any of that stuff to happen to them. They didn't want it, and they can't make it better. (*Still crying.*)

THERAPIST: Yeah. (*pause*) Now I'd like you to try to say to all three of them, "You are all lovable. You deserve good things. May you all be happy and safe."

PATRICK: (*Sobs for almost a minute.*) I just want to protect them.

THERAPIST: Yeah. That makes sense to me. (*pause*) Let's just stay here, especially focused on yourself as a 5-year-old boy. Let him know how much you love him and how you wish you could protect him.

PATRICK: I do.

THERAPIST: If you want, you can pick him up or say something to him.

PATRICK: "It's not your fault." (*Eyes still closed and crying.*)

We stayed with this scene for another 15 minutes or so, and Patrick's connection with his 5-year-old self deepened over that time. He became calmer and described feeling powerful warmth and love for that image of himself. At the end of the session, I told him to continue this new practice with the same diligence that he'd shown over the past week. I said that it might work to begin by picturing himself as a 5-year-old, but if it doesn't, he can use the same progression we used that day: First picture his niece, then the other boy, then himself as a boy.

Over the next 6 weeks, Patrick experienced an incredible amount of healing and transformation. It seemed like he had a new insight to report at the start of almost every session. He would tell me about an experience of abuse or neglect and how he no longer felt responsible for it or ashamed about it. He was grieving his childhood in a healthy way and moving forward in his life. In our last session, he said, "My anxiety and depression are basically gone, and I'm starting to feel like I could like myself for who I am. I'll call you if I need some help in the future."

Let's go back through that pivotal session with Patrick to highlight a few important points. At the beginning, when he asked if it would be possible to like himself more, I responded enthusiastically. As I mentioned in Chapter 3, one of the core elements of building a strong alliance is that the therapist and client both *believe* that therapy will help. I never want to promise that a client will definitely get better, because I can't guarantee that. However, it can give clients a lot of strength to know that change is possible and that many other people have experienced it.

Patrick wanted to let go of shame and self-criticism, which I knew had originated in his traumatic childhood. If the source of someone's suffering is in the past, then we want to send love and compassion to the past. Therefore, my goal was to help Patrick learn how to direct compassion to himself as a child. I started out by guiding him to picture his niece, a practice we had already learned could activate his Care Circuit. Then, while the oxytocin and opioids were flowing, I asked him to picture himself as a child in the hopes that he could embrace his younger self with the same compassion. However, when he reported strong negative feelings, I knew he wasn't yet ready for that step.

At that point, I had a few options. We could have just gone back and spent more time with his niece to see if deepening his experience of love and warmth for her would be enough to shift things. However, I had an intuition that it wouldn't be enough. He seemed to be blaming his 5-year-old self for the problems in his family, which created a formidable obstacle to compassion. I wanted him to see that his child self wasn't to blame, so I used a technique that is common to many forms of experiential therapy. I had him imagine someone else who had lived through similar experiences.

Happily, it wasn't too hard for Patrick to feel compassion for this other boy. When he said, "I wish you had a better life," I knew that he was feeling compassion. Then, when I pointed out the similarities between him and the other boy, there was no resistance. Finally, seeing those similarities, he could extend compassion to his childhood self as well.

When Patrick was connecting with his 5-year-old self, I suggested that he express how he wished he could protect that child. Clients respond very differently in situations like this, so I try to follow their lead. Some clients want to visualize intervening in an act of abuse or neglect. They imagine the scene as it was, and then have their adult self or another adult come in and rescue the child. Other clients imagine picking the child up and telling him or her, "I will protect you from now on." However, this isn't helpful for everyone. Some people find it upsetting and say, "This didn't really happen, so it can't help."

Therefore, I encourage clients to express their wish to be able to protect the child in whatever way makes sense to them. Any visualization is appropriate if it helps the client engage the Care Circuit while the painful memory is activated. That is the most important point.

In this example, we can see the power of directing compassion right at the source of someone's suffering. When Patrick pictured his niece, it was a preliminary practice for him to learn how to stimulate his Care Circuit. He was able to use this practice to regulate his emotions, but it didn't change the deeper cause of his issues. When he was able to send compassion directly to his childhood suffering, he experienced a deep transformation.

Chapter 8

WORKING WITH STUBBORN SELF-CRITICISM AND SELF-SABOTAGE

*"Love is the only force capable of transforming
an enemy into a friend."*
—Martin Luther King, Jr.
(1957, December)

Why are people so mean to themselves? At a recent seminar, a psychologist opened up about this issue in a particularly beautiful and vulnerable way. He said, "I really believe in self-compassion. I read Sharon Salzberg and Chris Germer, but every time I look in a mirror, I have the thought, 'I'm too fat and I hate my nose.' Why can't I stop judging and criticizing myself?"

We are a brilliant species, but we often act as our own worst enemies. We might know exactly what we need to do to achieve our goals and be happy, but we often get in our own way or just refuse to do it. How many of our clients are unwilling to fully engage with therapy or fail to heed advice that could change their lives for the better? How many desperately cling to self-destructive patterns in the face of our every attempt to help?

This is a serious problem and one of the biggest sources of frustration for therapists. In this chapter, I attempt to explain why these issues can be so stubborn and how self-compassion practices can break through this stagnation to create real change.

LOOKING FOR A HELPFUL THEORY

Psychologists and philosophers have attempted to explain self-criticism and self-sabotage with countless theories, but most of them create more problems than they solve, or conflict with what we know about the brain.

Some theories don't seem to account for this issue at all. They assume that irrational thoughts or behaviors are the result of plain ignorance. As soon as a client is taught how to think and act in a more adaptive way, positive change should follow. They have no explanation for people who cling to self-criticism or self-sabotage in the face of logic and reason.[1]

Then there are theories that originate with Plato and the Stoics[2] that claim our intellect is rational but our emotions are irrational (Montgomery, 1993). They seek to explain the apparent irrationality of self-criticism and self-sabotage by saying that those things belong to the domain of emotion, which can't be understood by the intellect. This kind of theory has almost no explanatory power because it just says that some things can't be explained. Although I believe there are plenty of things in the world that are beyond our understanding, I don't think this is one of them, and I attempt to show that below.

Other theories that originate with Freud and Nietzsche say that people have an innate urge to harm themselves that must be controlled using the will and social convention (Lind, 1991). However, from an evolutionary perspective, this doesn't seem to make sense. How could an urge like that benefit a species? Why would it develop? I hope to show that this kind of urge isn't necessary to explain self-criticism.

Biological psychiatrists have attempted to forward a theory that pathological thoughts and behaviors are caused by some dysfunctional biological system, possibly our neurotransmitters. However, despite spending millions of dollars over the past 40 years looking for evidence of such dysfunction, none has been found (Wyatt & Midkiff, 2006). As I mentioned in Chapter 2, many neuroscientists are rejecting this model and prefer to think in terms of implicit memories.

Finally, there are theories that claim self-criticism is caused by having been treated badly as a child. Some say it is a defense the child develops to survive the abuse. Others say the abuse "teaches" the child that he or she is bad. I believe this way of thinking is a good start, but it also fails to answer some important questions. For example, it makes a lot of sense that children blame themselves when they are abused. Piaget (1974) tells us that young children believe they cause everything that happens to them (and around them), because they haven't yet developed the cognitive ability to see that other people have their own motives and perspectives. However, this doesn't explain why these maladaptive beliefs would persist into adulthood. How is it possible for so many people to continue to blame themselves for abuse *after having learned* that children are not responsible for how they are treated?

Larry's Puzzling Problem

Imagine that a client named Larry comes to see you for therapy. He tells you about his violent inner critic and how he blames himself whenever anything goes wrong in his life. Then he explains that his parents were emotionally abusive and that he completely understands how he got his self-critical attitude. He says, "I know I internalized my parents' attacking voices, but just knowing that hasn't helped. I know I'm being irrational. I blame myself when I'm clearly not at fault. It's like my head knows I'm a good person, but my gut keeps telling me I'm not." Larry explains that he's seen several therapists over the past few years and that his problem is as bad as ever. How do we make sense out of this? What could help him?

It might be clear that Larry is carrying a lot of pain from his childhood and needs to do some healing. However, it's not clear why this issue has been so difficult to treat. I believe there are two concepts, discussed in the previous chapter, that can be extremely helpful in working with clients like this. The first is *modularity*, by which I mean having a deep appreciation for how the mind is made up of many different psychological parts. The second is *constructivism*, by which I mean focusing on the stories we create to make sense out of our experience, rather than just the objective events. When you put these two concepts together, you end up with a model that can shed some light on why Larry's self-criticism has been so resistant to therapy and what we could do to help him.

In the previous chapter I explained these two ideas to a level of detail that I believe would be acceptable to most cognitive scientists. Here I extend them to what I believe are their logical conclusions and articulate a theory that I hope can make sense out of stubborn self-criticism and self-sabotage. I call this theory *modular constructivism*.

MODULAR CONSTRUCTIVISM[3]

In Chapter 2, I discussed how our System 1, automatic thinking, creates stories to make sense out of our experiences. We construct these stories to explain *why* things happen in our lives. We do this automatically, immediately, and generally without conscious awareness. There is a strong consensus in cognitive science that System 1 creates stories to make sense out of absolutely every experience in our lives (Kahneman, 2011). Psychological constructivists are primarily interested in how these stories affect our mental health.[4]

When we apply this concept to Larry, it helps us understand the origins of his self-criticism. As he was growing up in an emotionally abusive home, Larry's System 1 had to create a story to make sense out of why his parents were so mean to him. Using the type of thinking that was developmentally appropriate for his age, his System 1 concluded: "My parents yell at me and demean me because I'm a bad kid." It did so without his conscious awareness, and that story began to affect how he interpreted other situations. If Larry's teacher yelled at him, he would likely believe she was doing it *because he was bad*. He might not be able to articulate that, but he would act as though it were his fault. Another child with more supportive parents who was also in Larry's class might have created a different story, such as, "My teacher yells because she's mean." This is basic constructivism, and I think it makes sense to most of us.

As Larry grew up, his style of thinking matured. He developed the ability to see that life's problems have lots of different causes. He is partially responsible for the issues in his life, and other people and random circumstance play a big role as well. This more mature part of him creates stories that are fairly realistic and well-adjusted. However, the development of this new part did not destroy, replace, or even substantially affect the younger part. They both continue to exist and create their own separate stories.

We can imagine that the younger part is made up of a certain network of neurons in his brain. The more mature part is made of a different neural network. These two networks are functionally separate and don't communicate.[5] They each create separate stories to make sense out of Larry's experience, and those different stories shape his emotional reality. To be clear, I'm not saying these parts *cannot* communicate. They will when we get deeper into therapy, but they haven't so far.

The younger part creates stories based on the assumption that Larry is bad. Whenever a difficult situation arises in his life—if he breaks a dish or gets into an argument with his girlfriend—that part will create a story that it happened *because he is bad*. The other part will have a more rational story. This is what I mean by *modular constructivism*: different parts (modularity) creating their own stories (constructivism).[6]

Working with Separate Parts and Separate Stories

If you want to help someone like Larry, one of the most important points to remember is that you will need to *direct compassion to the part of him that is causing his suffering*. In other words, you will be working with the younger part of him that believes he is bad. The more mature part of him—the part with which he usually identifies—already knows that he is lovable. The most likely reason Larry's previous therapists weren't more successful is that they were probably targeting their interventions at the wrong part of him.

What does it mean to target an intervention to one particular part of a client? In Chapter 2, I explained the process of memory reconsolidation. To review, if you want to transform a memory, you activate it and then expose it to new information. If you want to heal a distressing memory, you activate it and then send yourself compassion. Therefore, we want to activate that younger part of Larry and guide him through a self-compassion practice.

How do we go about "activating" Larry's younger part? In order to create deep change, Larry needs to get in touch with the thoughts, feelings, and bodily sensations associated with this younger part. The more vividly he connects with his younger part, the greater the possibility for transformation (Dębiec et al., 2006). Visualization is the most commonly used technique to accomplish this connection, but other experiential interventions are also possible.[7] Larry could visualize himself as a young child and have a conversation with that child. He could also imagine *being* that young child and talk with you from that state.

If you want to be sure you've successfully connected Larry with his younger part, there are two points to keep in mind. First, whatever visualization or other technique you are using must *elicit powerful emotions* in his body. Second, the thoughts and core beliefs associated with that part must *feel subjectively true* to him during the intervention. In other words, if Larry is reporting some kind of intense emotion in his body, and the sentence "I'm bad" feels subjectively true to him, then you have succeeded in helping him activate his younger part.

Making an Enemy into a Friend

Once you've helped Larry activate the younger part of him that believes he's bad, how can you use self-compassion to begin healing it? We might begin by guiding Larry to imagine being himself as a 6-year-old boy. If he reports feeling intense sadness and fear in the form of tension and heaviness in his whole body, and says it would feel true to say the sentence "I know that I'm bad," then we have completed the first step of activating his younger self. I discuss the details of those interventions a little later, but for now let's look at what happens next.

If you want to help Larry find compassion for his younger self, a great way to begin is by reflecting on what would help you to feel compassion for a child like that. Take a moment and imagine a 6-year-old child who comes from an emotionally volatile home. He tells you, "I'm a bad kid and that's why my mom and dad always yell at me. It's my fault." Let that image be really clear and notice how *you* feel in your body. Does it make you sad, angry, and/or do you feel a strong urge to comfort and support that child? Now that you understand modularity, you might notice you feel all three.

Focus on the part of you that feels compassion for little Larry and take a minute to deepen into that feeling. Let it get really strong. Then reflect on how you could express your compassion to him. Do you feel like giving him a hug, offering to protect him, or telling him that he's not a bad kid? Again, you might feel all three. Take another minute and imagine interacting with this sad little boy. Imagine expressing your compassion in different ways and notice how he responds. Are there particular things you say or do that seem to have a bigger effect on him?

Now I'd like you to reflect on this child in light of the *three key ingredients for compassion*:

1. *We understand the person suffers.* Make sure you recognize how this child is suffering (this is probably pretty obvious).
2. *We understand the person wants to be happy and is attempting (however unskillfully) to create happiness for self and others.* This might be a little more challenging. If he wants to be happy, then why does Larry blame himself? He would obviously prefer if his parents were kind and loving. When he blames himself, his intention is not to make things worse. He does it

because he has no other way to make sense out of why his parents would be so mean.

3. *We understand that we are not fundamentally separate from each other.* Finally, put yourself in his shoes. See if you can recognize that you might think the same way if you were a child in a situation like that.

Hopefully this process has helped you get in touch with compassion for the kind of child that Larry was. Once you feel clear about how to generate feelings of compassion for that child and how to express them in a way the child can appreciate, you will have a better chance to help Larry.

Sometimes expressing love and support will feel like the most powerful thing we can do. For example, Larry might imagine picking up the child, holding him, and telling him how much he is loved. However, sometimes the child part won't be able to accept love until he stops blaming himself for the abuse. In situations like this, he will need to create a different story to make sense out of what happened. It's almost impossible to let go of an old story until we have a new one to replace it. An old story always has a purpose, which is to explain *why* something happened. The new story will need to answer that question in a way that's at least as compelling as the old one.

If Larry's younger part was formed when he was around 6 years old, it will need an alternative story that makes sense to a child of that age. For example, "Your parents are not mean to you because you are bad. They are like that because other people have been mean to them, and they never learned how to be kind." Parts that were formed in childhood will continue to operate at the level of cognitive development from when they were formed.[8]

Whether you are trying to help his younger part create a new story or just sending it love and compassion, we can see there are a few concepts that are vital to helping Larry achieve real change. The first concept is *modularity*, which means you recognize that his inner critic is a relatively autonomous part. After hearing about his childhood, you could safely assume it was formed then. The second concept is *constructivism*, which means you assume that Larry's negative core beliefs were formed as his best attempt to make sense out of a painful experience. You know that he will need a story to make sense out of it, and you might have to help him create a new one. The third concept is *self-compassion*, which means that you recognize the healing power of helping Larry develop a compassionate and loving attitude toward this part of himself.

Most of us view self-criticism and self-sabotage as enemies that should be challenged and defeated, or at least ignored. In this case, we can see how deeper understanding can transform Larry's inner critic from an enemy into a child in need of love and compassion.

APPLYING MODULAR CONSTRUCTIVISM AND SELF-COMPASSION IN SESSIONS

Now that we've considered these key concepts, let's explore how they can be concretely applied in clinical work.

Continuing with Maria and Compassion for Self-Criticism

When Maria returned for her second session, she looked noticeably better. Her hair and clothes were clean, and she seemed less agitated. She told me she had been using the visualization of Jesus on the cross every day, and that it had given her a lot of peace. She still hadn't done anything to clean her house, but she had begun bathing and cooking for herself. She said this practice had given her more energy to get through the day, but her self-critical thoughts were as strong as ever. She was still adamant that she didn't deserve Christ's love.

We spent our second session revisiting her practice and talking about how she could use it to get her through difficult moments. This is a transcript from the next session (her third).

THERAPIST: What should we focus on today?
MARIA: I had another good week. I'm doing better.

THERAPIST: I'm glad to hear that. Do you want to tell me about some of the things that are going well or talk more about things you hope to change? We could also do some of both.

MARIA: I feel better after I do the compassion practice, but then I start thinking again and getting mad at myself. It's like that practice helps for a little while, but then I end up getting so mad at myself.

THERAPIST: OK. That makes sense. (*pause*) It sounds like there's a part of you that gets really mad at yourself. Would you like to try to see if we can understand that part a little better?

MARIA: Yeah, OK. Can you make it go away?

THERAPIST: I believe we will be able to make it better. (*She smiles.*) We just have to understand that part a little more before we can know what is going to help. Does that make sense?

MARIA: Yeah. So what do we do?

THERAPIST: Let's try an exercise and see if it helps. (*pause*) Do you feel mad at yourself right now? On a scale from 0 to 10, where 0 is not mad at all and 10 is the maddest you've ever been, what number would you give yourself now?

MARIA: Like *right* now? I guess, maybe a 2.

THERAPIST: Great. Thanks. What we are going to do next is bring up some of those angry thoughts for just a minute or so. We will bring them up so we can learn a little more about them. In my experience, this is really the best way to learn about a part like the one you're describing. Is that OK?

MARIA: I guess, if that's what you think will help.

THERAPIST: OK. Thanks. Can you tell me about the last time you got really mad at yourself?

MARIA: This morning before I came here. I woke up and did my compassion practice and felt pretty good. Then I went to go make coffee and the coffee maker was dirty and I started thinking, "You are good for nothing. You can't do anything. Look at this mess you made. You should be ashamed!"

THERAPIST: OK. That's perfect. Thank you. (*pause*) Now see if you can picture yourself back there, just for a minute. You can see that the coffee maker is dirty. (*pause*) Can you feel that part getting mad at you?

MARIA: (*Closes eyes.*) Yeah. I feel it.

THERAPIST: Good. What does it feel like in your body? Like, is there tension or heaviness or anything else like that?

MARIA: Yes. My whole body is tense, and I feel like I'm being crushed and choked.

THERAPIST: OK. Thanks. And while you are feeling that, what do the thoughts say?

MARIA: They say, "You are good for nothing. You should never have been born."

THERAPIST: OK. (*pause*) Now as you are feeling that tension in your body and feeling crushed and choked, can you think back to the first time you can remember feeling that way? It doesn't need to be the first time ever, just the first time in your life that you can remember feeling like this.

MARIA: Yes. I think I felt like this all the time when I was a girl. I think about times my parents were screaming at each other and screaming at me. I think about another time they left me alone, and I was so hungry. It was like, all the time.

THERAPIST: That makes sense. (*Speaking slowly with a lot of warmth.*) When you picture some of these scenes, how old is the girl in the scene?

MARIA: Maybe 6 or 7.

THERAPIST: OK. Let's choose one scene from when you were 6 or 7. We'll pick one scene where you really felt all of these feelings. Can you choose one?

MARIA: Yeah. The time I was alone and hungry. They told me they hated me and then left for the whole day. I didn't know if I would ever see them again. I was so scared.

THERAPIST: Thanks. [I'm aware we are getting into the realm of acute trauma, and I'm assessing her level of emotional arousal. I know the Jesus visualization could help if she becomes hyperaroused.] So see if you can picture that little girl who is alone and hungry and tell me when you can see her.

MARIA: I can see her.

THERAPIST: OK. I'd like for you to ask that little girl *why* she thinks this is happening to her and let me know what she says.

MARIA: She says, "I'm ugly and I'm good for nothing. I just get in the way."

THERAPIST: Thanks. (*pause*) When you hear this little girl say that, what are the feelings that come up for you, or what do you want to say to her?

MARIA: I want to cry. She is so sad and lonely.

THERAPIST: Why do *you* think this is happening to her?

MARIA: I don't know. She's just a little girl.

THERAPIST: Yeah. She's just a little girl. (*pause*) Let's slow down and pause here. I want you to keep picturing this scared little girl. She thinks that the reason her parents have done this to her is that she's "good for nothing," but you can see she's just a scared little girl. Let me know what thoughts and feelings come up as you reflect on this.

MARIA: (*Eyes still closed.*) She didn't do anything wrong. (*Starts to cry.*)

THERAPIST: That's right. She didn't do anything wrong. (*Pause until her crying slows down.*) You see that really clearly. She didn't do anything wrong, and she's just a scared little girl. Now we need to help her understand *why* her parents did this so she won't keep blaming herself.

MARIA: Yes!

THERAPIST: Good. So if she hasn't done anything wrong and she is just a little girl, why would her parents treat her this way? If we know it is *not the girl's fault*, then why is it happening?

MARIA: (*Puts her head in her hands, eyes still closed.*) I don't know. Her parents must be monsters. (*Shifts from sadness to anger.*) I hate them.

THERAPIST: That's one possibility. To treat a little girl who hasn't done anything wrong like this is hard to understand. It makes them seem like monsters. (*pause*) We don't know why they are like this. Maybe no one ever loved them. I don't know. What is really clear is that the girl is not to blame.

MARIA: Yes! That is clear.

THERAPIST: Now, I'd like to you to explain this to the little girl. Tell her that it's not her fault. Her parents are cruel, and we don't know why.

MARIA: I know why. My father was almost beaten to death by his father several times. My mother's family was very poor, and she was afraid of my father.

THERAPIST: OK. You can explain all of that to the little girl. Tell her it isn't her fault.

MARIA: And I want to tell her I'm sorry this happened to her and I love her.

THERAPIST: Yes. Tell her that too.

MARIA: (*Long pause while crying softly.*) She believes me. I feel like I need to sleep.

THERAPIST: Yeah. That makes sense. This is a lot of work.

I continued to validate how tiring this kind of work can be and told her to rest a lot over the coming week. I suggested that she picture that 6-year-old girl every day and continue connecting with her. I wrote some notes to remind her about how to practice, including the importance of telling the girl that she's not to blame for the abuse and explaining the real reasons her parents acted like that, as well as continuing to express love and affection to the girl. Finally, I said, "You might also try picturing Jesus sending love to both you—as an adult and as a little girl."

Over the next few weeks, we developed some practices for her to use whenever negative thoughts arose in her daily life. When she started having self-critical thoughts, she would imagine they were coming from this little girl. Then she could respond by telling the girl things like, "I know you feel like that because of how your parents treat you. You are really a beautiful girl and I love you." Within 2 months, she had experienced a radical transformation. Her day-to-day thinking had become relatively self-compassionate and when negative thoughts did arise, she could care for them. It took a lot longer for her to build up skills for taking care of herself and communicating with others, but she made steady progress. This is what I mean by turning the inner critic from an enemy into a friend.

Returning to the transcript, we can see that she initially described her experience as "getting mad at myself." I reflected that back in the language of parts by saying, "There's a part of you that gets really mad at yourself." This helped her begin to disidentify with those harmful thoughts and helped me explain the value of learning about that part.

Next, we "activated" that part by having her imagine a recent time she had gotten mad at herself. I knew that part was activated because she described powerful feelings in her body, and the negative statements felt subjectively true to her. At this point, I knew almost nothing about her inner critic. However, modular constructivism would predict that it was formed by trying to make sense out of some painful experience in the past.

The next intervention I used was designed to uncover the circumstances that had led to that part's formation. I asked her to describe the first time she could remember feeling that way, and the exercise gave me a clear picture of how her self-critical narrative was formed. For this kind of intervention to be effective, her inner critic must be experientially activated.

When she described her life as a young girl, I had to send myself a lot of compassion in order to stay present with her. I could feel my own sadness growing and knew that I did not want to be overwhelmed by it. I took a few breaths and practiced self-compassion until I found some peace. I silently told myself, "It's OK to feel sad about this—you wish no child were ever treated like this," and that helped prevent me from getting lost in my own countertransference.

We had now connected with the part of her that was suffering and in need of love. At this point, we could have just attempted to send some compassion to that little girl. It could have come from herself as an adult, from Jesus, or another source. However, I thought this girl might have become defensive if someone just started showering her with love. She might need a different way to make sense out of her abuse before she could let it in. If we had tried sending her compassion at this point, the girl might not have trusted those expressions of affection or even responded with anger.

Once a client has connected with the part of him- or herself that is suffering, sometimes just sending compassion to that part is entirely sufficient. Other clients who have a powerful story that they are not worthy of love will often need to replace that story before they can let compassion in. Finally, some clients will need more help letting go of their negative story, because the alternative story creates new problems. (I explain this point more fully in the next example.)

After she had a dialogue with that 6-year-old girl and explained why she was not to blame for her parents' actions, Maria began to feel an overwhelming amount of love and warmth for her. That spontaneous expression of compassion for the part of her that suffered is exactly what I'm hoping for when working with self-criticism.

Working with Chris and Self-Sabotage

Chris, a mechanical engineer in his mid 30s, had seen nine different therapists over the past 7 years before coming to me. He struggled with depression and anger that had impacted his career, and he was almost completely socially isolated. One of the first things he said to me was, "I read that you studied with Thich Nhat Hanh. I think I need to learn mindfulness, and I think *you* are the one who is going to be able to help me." His immediate confidence in me after having fired so many other therapists was a red flag, and I thought he was likely to feel disappointed with me before long.

That turned out to be true. Our first two sessions followed a pattern like this: He expressed something he wanted to change about himself, I asked if he'd like to try a practice to see if it would help, he asked me to explain the practice and then told me why it couldn't possibly help him. When I asked if he would prefer just talking with me about his life and his past, he said, "I've done too much of that with other therapists and it doesn't help. I need something concrete." Over those first 2 hours, we seemed to cover a huge spectrum of possible interventions from many different orientations. We were primarily focused on Buddhist psychology, but also discussed behaviorism, CBT, expressive therapies, and even psychodynamics. He told me he had already tried some of those interventions and that he believed the others had no chance of helping him. When I recommended we actually try experimenting with a few practices rather than just discussing them, he said he didn't want to waste time on things he knew wouldn't help.

In our third session, I took a little more control. I told him that the way that I prefer to assess interventions is to actually try them out, and I understood if he wanted to look for a different therapist. After 10 or 15 minutes of debate, he agreed to try mindfulness of the body for his depression. Using Dialogue-Based Mindfulness, I guided him to feel his depression as sensations in his body and to welcome it with open acceptance. He reported his sadness had gone from an 8 out of 10 to a zero by the end of that exercise and said, "I actually feel pretty peaceful. You are amazing." I wrote out some instructions for him to practice on his own, and he assured me he would practice every day.

When he arrived for his next session, I asked how his week had gone and if he had been able to practice mindfulness by himself. He immediately launched into a speech about having realized after he left the session that the exercise hadn't actually helped him at all, or at least couldn't be useful going forward. He said we needed to come up with something different.

I considered the possibility that he had been trying to please me in the last session and hadn't actually benefitted from the practice. However, it just didn't ring true. I was getting the feeling that some part of him was trying to sabotage therapy, so I decided to test that hypothesis. This transcript is from the middle of our fourth session.

THERAPIST: Sure. We can try something different, but remember I actually want to try it out rather than just talking about it.

CHRIS: Yeah. That's fine. That's just the way you work.

THERAPIST: OK. So let's focus on depression again—that heavy, sinking feeling in your gut [that was how he had described it the week before]. Are you feeling that now?

CHRIS: A little, yeah.

THERAPIST: When is the last time it was really strong?

CHRIS: Last night I got home after work and ate a whole pizza and stayed up until 3 A.M. playing video games. A friend had invited me to a dinner party, and I didn't even call him back.

THERAPIST: OK. Can you picture yourself back there? Let me know when you can see yourself there.

CHRIS: (*Closes eyes.*) Yeah. I'm there.

THERAPIST: Do you feel that heavy sinking feeling in your gut?

CHRIS: (*painful expression on face*) Oh, I hate it. It is the worst.

THERAPIST: OK. So while you're feeling it, I'm going to give you a sentence to complete. I'll give you the beginning of a sentence, and you will just say the first thing that pops into your head. It doesn't even need to make sense—just whatever pops up. We'll do it a few times. Does that make sense?

CHRIS: Sure.

THERAPIST: You are feeling that heavy, sinking feeling in your gut and you're home alone eating pizza and playing video games. Now picture some of the most important people in your life and finish the sentence, "I need to stay depressed because if I don't . . ." What pops up?

CHRIS: I need to stay depressed because if I don't . . . ugggh.

THERAPIST: OK. Let's do it again—just whatever pops into your head.

CHRIS: I need to stay depressed because if I don't, you're going to get away with it. (*loud sigh*)

THERAPIST: Who will?

CHRIS: My [expletive] parents.

THERAPIST: Let's say it again. I need to stay depressed because if I don't, you're going to get away with it. How do they get away with it?

CHRIS: You will never admit how bad you were.

THERAPIST: Great. Say that directly to them. Picture your parents there and try saying, "I need to stay depressed because if I don't, you will never have to admit how bad you were." You can say it out loud or silently to yourself. Just try saying it a few times and let me know what comes up.

CHRIS: (*Long pause while he repeats the sentence silently.*) They are just horrible people.

THERAPIST: I believe you. (*pause*) Now picture them and let me know what you wish they would admit. What could they say that would feel really powerful?

CHRIS: I just want them to say they are bad people and treated me like [expletive]. I want them to walk around with a huge sign that says, "We were bad parents and we know it." But they act like they were these saints and pretend they care. It's so phony.

THERAPIST: Yeah. You just want them to admit the truth.

CHRIS: Exactly!

THERAPIST: And they won't.

CHRIS: I know.

THERAPIST: And your only chance to make them admit it is to stay depressed and alone. Is that right?

CHRIS: If my life is bad enough, they will have to admit they were not the perfect parents. It sounds crazy, but it's true.

THERAPIST: It doesn't sound crazy to me. It sounds like there is a part of you that wants your parents to admit how bad they were. That part wants it so badly that it's willing to make you depressed forever.

CHRIS: (*Starts crying.*) I don't want to be depressed forever.

THERAPIST: Yeah. That part is true also. You hate being depressed and alone. One part of you thinks the most important thing is to stop being depressed, but another part says it's more important to make your parents admit how bad they were. Does that sound right?

CHRIS: Yeah. That's it. (*another long sigh*) So what do I do?

THERAPIST: For now, all I want you to do is to remember that these parts exist, and it's important that you don't take sides. Both of these parts have important things to say. If you can recognize this conflict in you and not turn one side into the enemy, you will feel better soon.

I wrote the core insight from this session on a notecard and told him to read it at least twice a day. It said, "One part of me thinks the most important thing in the world is to get my parents to admit how bad they were. That part believes my only chance is to stay really depressed. Another part of me sees how much this depression is hurting me and wants to stop. Both parts are trying to meet an important need, and neither one is the enemy."

When Chris returned the next week, the first thing he said was, "I gave up. I don't think they will ever admit it, even if I kill myself. It feels incredibly unfair and makes me angry, but I'm not willing to keep being depressed anymore. It's just not worth it." He described how letting go of this attachment had helped him begin to see his life completely differently. He recognized that so many of his self-destructive behaviors were about defending his depression and he no longer felt attracted to any of them. He said, "I see it now and I can't believe I didn't see it before. That part of me really *wanted* to stay depressed. It was committed to shooting holes in anything that might have actually made me feel better."

Over the next five sessions, Chris wrestled with many different feelings and made rapid progress. He expressed how unfair it felt that his parents would never admit how badly they had treated him, but I helped him see that if he could let himself grieve, he could let that go. He also talked about feeling ashamed for keeping himself depressed for so long. We practiced the three key ingredients of compassion for that part of him, especially focused on the second: *We understand the person (or part) wants to be happy and is attempting (however unskillfully) to create happiness.* He was eventually able to see that this part of him actually wanted him to be happy and believed the only way to be truly happy was to force his parents to admit their wrongs. By the end of Session 9, he was taking care of himself and engaging in lots of positive habits. He said he didn't think he needed therapy anymore and would be in touch if things got worse. I get a card from him every Christmas saying that his life is going really well and thanking me for our work together.

Now let's return to the transcript. Based on his history and our first three sessions, I was curious if some part of him was trying to sabotage therapy. However, I certainly wasn't sure this was true. I needed to test that hypothesis. In situations like this one, Robert Kegan's concept of *competing commitments* has had a huge influence on me. Kegan describes how it's possible for someone to have two conflicting goals simultaneously (Kegan & Lahey, 2001).

I knew that a big part of Chris wanted to get better. He had invested a huge amount of time and energy toward that end. However, what if some part of him did not? What if that part actively wanted to stay depressed? I had no idea why it might want that, but I knew it was possible and could explain his behaviors. I love Kegan's concept so much because it helps us find compassion for even the most seemingly dysfunctional parts of ourselves. It reminds us that even self-sabotage can be an attempt to avoid suffering and create happiness.

From the start of this session, I was actively looking for a competing commitment. I wasn't positive I'd find one, but I wanted to test and see if one was there. Was there a part of him that wanted to remain depressed? Again, to do this kind of "parts work," we have to start by activating the part that is creating the symptom. I had him picture himself in a scene that activated his depression in order to test whether there might be a part of him that didn't want to let it go.

Once his depression was activated, I used a sentence completion to look for competing commitments. Kegan and Lahey (2001) have a structured interview that they like to use, but I've found there are many different interventions that can work here. I review several specific interventions below.

I asked Chris to picture any important people from his life because I assumed that his purpose for holding onto depression might relate to a core relationship. In my experience, this is often the case. The instructions for the sentence completion were to let me know whatever words popped into his head, even if they didn't make sense. I'm hoping the self-sabotaging part will complete the sentence, and I'm aware that whatever words it would use might sound crazy to his conscious self.

The trick to a good sentence completion is to get the right part of the client to respond to your prompt. You want to make sure the part you are looking for is highly activated or the client might respond, "I *don't* need to stay depressed—I want to get rid of this more than anything." With Chris, if this intervention hadn't been productive, I would have just rephrased the sentence completion or tried a different technique. I'm usually willing to spend at least half a session looking for a competing commitment before I give up and return to more standard therapy.

Once he responded to the sentence completion, the rest of the session was about clarifying that part's exact purpose for wanting to stay depressed. We learned there was a part of him that believed the most important thing in the world would be to get his parents to admit their faults, and his best chance of making that happen was by remaining depressed. At the beginning of the session, Chris believed that his depression was something that *happened to him*. He tried to fight it and was unable to win. By the end of the session, he had made direct contact with the part of him that vehemently wanted to stay depressed for an important reason.

Self-compassion is a practice of deep nonviolence. We do not turn our own thoughts and feelings into enemies that must be destroyed. Instead, we use compassion and love to transform those enemies into friends. We listen, empathize, dialogue, and reconcile. Therefore, once Chris had listened to that part of himself, I wanted to make sure he didn't turn it into an enemy.

By the time Chris returned for his next session, that part had already been well integrated. He was consciously aware of wanting his parents to admit how badly they had treated him. He knew he had been choosing to stay depressed for that reason, and that his strategy was very unlikely to work. This integration led to profound changes in his life.

Let's reflect on Chris's case from the perspective of modular constructivism. Remember, *modular constructivism* means multiple parts creating different stories. The part of Chris that wanted to remain depressed was likely formed when he was a child or teen-

154 • SELF-COMPASSION IN PSYCHOTHERAPY

ager, judging from its level of cognitive development. "I will punish myself to teach you a lesson" sounds like the logic of late elementary school or early teenage years to me. At that time, Chris's parents weren't showing him the love and respect he wanted, and he didn't know how to change that. He was particularly offended by how they tried to present themselves as ideal parents to others. Therefore, his System 1 created the story, "If I seem depressed enough, they will have to admit they are bad parents." It was probably related to the hope, "If they admit they've been bad parents to me, they will have to change." These stories were not merely System 1's best attempt to make sense out of his situation. They were stories that had a *purpose*, which was to make his present suffering more palatable. Just like Larry and Maria, as Chris got older and his thinking matured, this younger part continued to assert its story outside of his conscious awareness. Once we discovered that part and empathized with its goals, the conflict was resolved and the result was deep healing.

COMMON PURPOSES FOR SELF-CRITICISM

What are some common purposes for sabotaging self-compassion? Most people who develop self-criticism were mistreated in some way as a child, and their System 1 created the narrative that they are bad to explain what happened. The following list describes some common purposes clients may have for resisting self-compassion.

- *Maintaining connection*. If I realize that I never deserved to be abused, then my parents become horrible people. If I deserved the abuse, I can continue feeling connected with them.
- *Maintaining the illusion of control*. If I am to blame for the abuse, then I can control it by becoming better. If I'm not to blame, then it is entirely outside of my control—and that is scary.
- *Maintaining fairness*. If I'm not to blame for the abuse, then I live in a world in which good people can be hurt without having done anything wrong. That would feel too unfair.

- *Protecting a relationship.* If I know that I am lovable, someone important in my life will reject me. This person believes that I deserve disrespect and could not tolerate it if I were to disagree.
- *Avoiding responsibility for life.* If I know there is nothing wrong with me, I become responsible for my life. Believing I'm broken allows me to escape responsibility.

SPECIFIC TECHNIQUES FOR IDENTIFYING AND WORKING WITH SELF-SABOTAGE

If a client is particularly stuck or uncooperative, there might be a part of him or her that actually *doesn't want* the therapy to succeed. If we can understand and empathize with that part of the client, real transformation is possible. This section explores how to identify whether a client might be engaging in self-sabotage and describes concrete steps for working with it.

The first step for successfully treating self-sabotage is to understand how it works. You know that self-sabotage can occur even when someone feels intensely motivated to change. Thinking in terms of the different parts of the client, you know there is a conscious part that wants to change and another part that has an important purpose for not changing. It is likely that the client is completely unaware that this second part exists. You aren't trying to destroy or defeat that part, but to understand and empathize with it.

If nothing you do seems to be helping a client, how can you tell if he or she might be engaging in self-sabotage? In my experience, the only way to truly know if a client is engaging in self-sabotage is to test for it experientially, which I explain below. We might suspect that self-sabotage is present, but we can't really know until the client discovers his or her own hidden purpose for holding onto the symptom. However, there are a few indicators that can alert us to the possibility that self-sabotage might be playing a role. For example:

- Seeming confident or comfortable with the notion that nothing will help.
- Being unwilling to commit to a therapy goal.
- Seeming ambivalent about change.
- Expressing something like, "I know what I need to do to feel better, but I can't get myself to do it."
- Being generally unresponsive to therapy.

If you suspect that self-sabotage might be present, but don't know for sure, you start by activating the symptom as vividly as possible (being careful not to overwhelm the client). Once the symptom is active, here are some techniques to use for discovering its hidden purpose.

- *Sentence completion.* This technique is commonly used in personality testing, but it can be a powerful discovery tool in therapy. This is the technique I used with Chris. The therapist gives the client the beginning of a sentence (called a *stem*) that the client completes with whatever comes to mind. We create a sentence stem that is designed to elicit the hidden purpose of the symptom. It can be phrased in terms of the positive desire to keep the symptom, such as, "I need to stay depressed because . . ." or in terms of not wanting to lose the symptom, "I refuse to let go of my anxiety, because if I do. . . ."

  Sometimes we need to do a series of sentence completions to fully uncover the purpose of a symptom. For example, an initial sentence completion might elicit the response, "I need to be depressed because if I'm not, I'll be normal." This wording reveals part of the purpose for being depressed, but it is still unclear why the client doesn't want to be normal. When we have fully uncovered the purpose for a symptom, it will pertain to a need that is *at least as vital* as the one threatened by the symptom. So we create another sentence completion that brings us to, "I refuse to be normal because normal people aren't special." We are closer, but one more iteration will make it even clearer. The final sentence completion arrives at, "I need to be special because that is the only way to be worthy of love." Now we really understand why staying depressed is worth such intense suffering.

- *Competing commitments interview.* Robert Kegan uses a structured interview to assess for self-sabotage (Kegan & Lahey, 2001). Table 8.1 is my adaptation of his interview, in which I've included sample answers and comments.

TABLE 8.1. Competing Commitments Interview

	Question	Answer	My Commentary
1	"What is your goal for therapy?"	"Have less anxiety."	Standard question
2	"What commitments does that goal imply?"	"Practicing relaxation and not thinking catastrophic thoughts."	This question helps us to be more concrete about what the client *could be doing* to create change. If the client doesn't know what to do or how to do it, then teaching new skills should be your focus here.
3	"What are you doing [or not doing] that is getting in the way of achieving your goal?"	"I have catastrophic thoughts often."	Many clients would say that these thoughts or feelings *happen to them*, rather than viewing them as something that *they do*. The trick here is to creatively help the client identify the ways he or she contributes to the problem.

4	"Imagine doing the opposite of the undermining behavior. Do you notice any discomfort, worry, or fear?"	"If I stop thinking about everything that might go wrong, I will be blindsided when it does."	This question is the key to this intervention. It helps the client recognize ambivalence by imagining what it would feel like to stop the undermining behavior. To do this requires a significant level of self-awareness, and clients who are not very self-aware might respond better to some of the other techniques described in this section.
5	"By engaging in your undermining behaviors, what problem are you preventing?"	"I prevent my being blindsided by an unexpected crisis."	This answer clarifies the information from the previous question and states it in terms of a positive intention.
6	"Is there an irrational assumption that is contributing to your undermining behavior?"	"Worrying about a crisis is the best way to prepare for it. It is better than being calm and grounded."	Usually, the therapist will have to help the client identify this assumption. It can be helpful to put yourself in the client's shoes. Imagine really believing the client's answer to Question 5. Take a moment to feel that in your body. Now reflect on how you would approach the situation differently.

- *Using the Feeding Your Demons™ process.* The Tibetan Buddhist teacher Tsultrim Allione (2008) teaches another wonderful process for identifying and bringing compassion to self-sabotage. This process begins by activating the symptom and feeling it in the body. Then the client personifies it in some humanoid form. For example, a client might imagine her self-criticism as a red devil with horns. The client is guided through a process of trying to empathize with this personification. Allione uses a very specific process, but it's possible to improvise here until you discover something that works for your client. Picturing the demon, the client can ask it questions like, "What do you need?"; "How are you trying to help?"; "What is your job?"; "What do you need me to hear?" You want to continue deepening the inquiry until the demon expresses the positive intention that is at the root of its actions.
- *Body dialogue.* In this technique, the client experiences the symptom as a sensation in the body. Instead of self-criticism appearing as a devil with horns, it might be an aching pain in the abdomen. The dialogue is the same as in the Feeding Your Demons™ process. You ask questions that seek to expose the positive intention in the symptom, and respond with compassion.
- *Other interventions.* Many experiential interventions can be adapted for working with self-sabotage. Gestalt, internal family systems, emotionally focused therapy, and many other forms of therapy have excellent interventions to offer.

Chapter 9

SPECIAL CASES

Treating Trauma, Addiction, and Psychosis

I believe the practices described in this book can be applied effectively to almost any clinical situation. However, some require special considerations. This chapter gives more specific guidance about how to use mindfulness and self-compassion practices with people who have experienced trauma, addiction, or psychosis.

TRAUMA: TRANSFORMING STRESS AND PROMOTING GROWTH

There is a saying in Buddhism that all compassion comes from suffering, and that great compassion comes from great suffering. Thich Nhat Hanh and the Dalai Lama are both symbols of great compassion for many people, and they are both survivors of trauma. They are war refugees (from Vietnam and Tibet, respectively) who have seen many of their close friends die violent deaths. Thich Nhat Hanh grew up during the French–Vietnamese war and grew into adulthood during the American–Vietnamese war. Some of his dearest friends were monks who set themselves on fire to protest the violence.

The Dalai Lama witnessed horrendous acts of violence when China invaded Tibet, including the brutal deaths of countless civilians and the destruction of sacred temples. Both of these monks are living proof of the capacity of mindfulness and compassion to transform trauma into kindness and strength. In this section, I discuss the benefits of using these practices with people who have experienced trauma, as well as some of the ways the practices can be adapted for this special population.

Self-compassion practices can be integrated into any form of trauma therapy, including EMDR, Somatic Experiencing®, and exposure. There are at least three elements that are common to all of these methods: a preparation stage, the task of monitoring the client's level of emotional arousal, and an explicit reprocessing stage. I'll discuss how self-compassion relates to each.

First, almost every trauma protocol includes some preparation work in which the client develops a basic capacity to relax and regulate emotions. Self-compassion practices are an excellent choice for this kind of work because they are an effective way of activating the Care Circuit in the brain, which powerfully reduces emotional distress.

Second, trauma therapies always require the therapist to monitor the client's level of emotional arousal to ensure that he or she doesn't become hyperaroused. We know that if a client triggers a fight–flight–freeze response during therapy, it can lead to retraumatization; this awareness is absolutely essential when using mindfulness and self-compassion with trauma.

The analogy that Thich Nhat Hanh uses when discussing this dynamic is about salt and water. If you were to drop a handful of salt into a glass of water, it would become undrinkable. However, if you drop the same amount of salt into a lake, the water would be perfectly fine. He explains that if your mindfulness and compassion are as small as a glass of water, your suffering will overwhelm you. If you can develop mindfulness and compassion that are as big as a lake, you can contain and embrace that suffering without being harmed by it.

Third, these methods all contain a reprocessing stage in which traumatic memories are activated in the therapy session. An understanding of memory reconsolidation can help clarify how this process works. As discussed earlier, reconsolidation occurs when we activate a memory and expose it to new associations. Practitioners of any trauma therapy will recognize this description as being a big part of what they do. However, a lot of trauma work achieves desensitization by activating the traumatic memory and associating it with a relatively neutral environment. If we could activate the memory and associate it with *compassion* instead, we could potentially expect superior results. Panksepp specifically talks about the transformative power of turning on the Care (or Play) Circuit in the brain while activating a distressing memory (Panksepp & Biven, 2012). A Buddhist might describe this process as getting in touch with our suffering and sending it compassion. A neuroscientist might describe the same process as activating a distressing memory while turning on the Care Circuit.

Most trauma methodologies engage the Care Circuit during reprocessing by having the therapist provide a caring and empathic environment. This is obviously an important part of any successful therapy. However, specific self-compassion practices like those described earlier in this book can often activate the Care Circuit even more powerfully than being in the presence of an empathic therapist.

Finally, many (but not all) trauma therapies seek to change clients' narratives about their traumas. Researchers who study loss and trauma talk about the central importance of the story we use to make sense out of a traumatic experience. In fact, the narrative we create about a trauma actually predicts the development of symptoms better than the intensity of the event itself (Neimeyer, 2006). For example, imagine two different people who were mugged in the same park. The first person creates a narrative that the world is a fundamentally unsafe place and anyone can become a victim anywhere. The second person interprets the experience as a wake-up call to organize his neighbors and make the neighborhood a safer place. It's almost certain the second person will have fewer traumatic symptoms than the first.

This is also why one person could merely witness a robbery—for example, being in a convenience store when it is robbed—and develop full-blown posttraumatic stress disorder (PTSD). Nothing directly happened to the witness, but he might be too afraid to leave the house for a year. On the other hand, someone could live through the Holocaust or a Tibetan monk could be tortured by Chinese soldiers and come through the experience relatively unscathed. It is the meaning attributed to the experience that makes all the difference.

Viktor Frankl (1961) articulates this insight beautifully in his reflections about his experience as a Holocaust survivor. His core message is that the meaning we create is more important than the circumstances of our lives, even in the face of trauma. He notes, "Between stimulus and response, there is a space" (p. 122). That space, which mediates our response, is filled with the meaning we create. While Frankl emphasizes our ability to choose our narratives, I believe it's important to remember that most narratives are initially created by System 1, automatically and outside of our awareness. They can be changed, but it's not easy.

Trauma Example: Jason and Childhood Sexual Abuse

Jason was sexually abused by his mother's boyfriend from the time he was 6 until he was 8. When his mother finally discovered what was happening, she left the boyfriend but refused to talk about it with Jason at all. With no support or guidance, he was left to process what had happened to him on his own. Jason got in trouble a lot at school, but eventually made it through college, and came to see me soon after he graduated.

Jason didn't disclose his abuse history right away. In our first session, he told me he had just ended his first long-term relationship and was blaming himself for the breakup. He said he needed to learn how to control his anger, so we spent our first few sessions focused on practicing mindfulness and self-compassion for that part of him. Eventually, he said there was a bigger reason why he was so angry and that it had caused other problems in his relationship as well. He told me about the abuse and said that he often experienced flashbacks during sex. He described other common symptoms of PTSD, including irritability, avoiding sex, and low self-esteem. He said he wanted to move on with his life and not have the abuse affect him so much.

We started this second phase of therapy with an amended form of compassion meditation, similar to what I described in Chapter 6. I asked Jason to explore different images until he found one that brought up feelings of *safety*, instead of warmth and love. Loving feelings can be a trigger for some people who have experienced sexual abuse, so I often focus on safety instead. The image he chose was his dog, and he practiced focusing on it until he was feeling peaceful and solid. We talked about how this practice could help him regulate negative emotions, and I recommended that he practice it as much as possible (20 minutes a day is good, an hour is better, and so on). I also explained that this practice would be helpful if he starts to get overwhelmed when we begin processing painful memories. In other words, it can be used in a way that's similar to how EMDR uses relaxation techniques.

After a few weeks of refining this practice and building more trust, we began working through some of his traumatic memories. This transcript begins after we had already done 10 minutes of meditation focusing on his dog, and Jason was feeling stable and calm.

THERAPIST: Now I'd like you to try picturing yourself as a little boy when you were around 6 or 7—just an image of that boy by himself. When you can see him there, let me know what feelings come up or what you want to say to him.

JASON: (*Eyes closed.*) I just feel rage. I want to scream at him for not standing up for himself. He's so weak and pathetic.

THERAPIST: OK. Thanks. (*pause*) Now we're going to change the image. See if you can picture a different little boy. He is around 7 years old, but it's not you. It's a different boy. Can you picture him?

JASON: Sure.

THERAPIST: This other little boy lived through abuse that was a lot like what you lived through. He is by himself, and he looks sad and lonely. Can you picture that?

JASON: Yeah.

THERAPIST: Knowing what he's lived through and how alone he feels, is there anything you'd like to say to him or any feelings that come up for you?

JASON: (*deep sigh*) I just feel bad for him. I don't know what to say.

THERAPIST: OK. We're just going to stay here with this image for a little while. (*pause*) You see this little boy who has been abused like you were, and you feel really bad for him. Do you feel bad for him because he's so small and there's nothing he could have done to protect himself?

JASON: Yeah. (*Face becomes very tense and breathing quickens.*)

THERAPIST: Now bring your dog into the image. Your dog is there too. You might decide to have your dog there alone, or it might be your dog and the little boy together. Let me know what you see.

JASON: My dog is playing with the boy, and it makes him happier. (*Tension seems to lessen and breathing slows.*)

THERAPIST: Let's just stay with this image for a while. You see how your dog can make everyone feel better. (*long pause*) Let me know if there's anything you feel like saying to the boy or any sensations you notice in your body.

JASON: I just want to tell him it's not his fault.

THERAPIST: Good. Tell him that and keep your dog there in the scene. Would it also feel true to tell him that it's going to end, and someday he will find a way to heal?

JASON: Yeah. I can say that.

THERAPIST: Let's stay with this for a little while. (*long pause*) Now I'd like for you to see if it's possible to imagine yourself as a little boy joining this other boy and your dog. Can you see that?

JASON: Yeah.

THERAPIST: And can you see how those two little boys have had really similar experiences? You just told the other little boy that what happened to him isn't his fault. Can you see that they both lived through the same things?

JASON: (*Long pause as his breathing gets very fast and his face tenses; doesn't respond for more than 30 seconds.*)

THERAPIST: Now shift your focus just to seeing your dog. Your dog is there by himself. Can you see your dog there?

JASON: Yeah. (*Breathing slows and deepens.*)

THERAPIST: Stay with that image of your dog and let me know if you're feeling any tension or heaviness or any other sensations in your body.

JASON: I'm starting to relax a little. I think I got pretty tense for a second. [We stay with the image of the dog alone for a few minutes. We don't move on until he reports feeling stable and calm.]

THERAPIST: Now we're going to experiment with picturing those two boys again. If it's too hard, we can just let it go. But let's see if you can come back to those two boys.

JASON: I can. I see them, and you're right. Neither of them deserved it. (*Starts crying and is unable to speak for almost a minute.*) "You don't deserve this! You are not a bad kid!" (*Opens his eyes and looks at me.*) I didn't do anything wrong!

THERAPIST: I know (*powerful eye contact for several seconds*). You were a little boy, and no one was there to protect you, but you are taking control of your life now and you're getting the support you need.

This session began a profound grieving process for Jason. There was a huge emotional release that started when he said, "Neither of them deserved it," and continued for several weeks. That moment in our session marked a major shift in his life. He stopped blaming himself for what had happened and began to grieve for his lost childhood. We developed a practice for him to send compassion to himself in the present and to his 7-year-old self. Just 2 weeks after this session, he found a 5-day meditation retreat nearby and did this practice for several hours each day. During the retreat, he checked in with me over the phone and described a remarkable depth of healing. He said: "It's like all that anger is gone. I don't really know how it happened, but I just don't hate myself like I used to. I feel sad sometimes, but it feels like a healthy kind of sad—not hopeless. For the first time in my life, I think I'm going to be OK." There was a lot more processing to do, and we continued therapy for another 3 months after the retreat, but Jason had truly begun to transform.

Now I'll go back through the transcript and comment on a few points. We began the session by focusing on Jason's dog until he felt peaceful and calm. I always want a client to be as grounded as possible before bringing up traumatic material. I also want to make sure that whatever centering practice we've created for the client is still effective, since a certain exercise might be powerful one week and ineffective the next.

I asked him to picture himself as a child to assess his attitudes toward that part of himself. I specifically said that the child was alone to make sure he didn't picture an act of abuse, which I assumed would have been overwhelming for him. At that point, I didn't know how he would react. He might have responded with compassion or at least pity for the child. If he had, we would have focused on finding ways to express that compassion. On the other hand, if he had been overcome with sadness, we could have used the image of his dog to regulate his emotions and then checked to see if that sadness was connected to compassion. However, what Jason actually expressed was anger and blaming toward himself as a little boy.

At that point, I knew Jason could feel compassion for his dog but not for himself as a little boy. I wanted to find some way to help him bring compassion and forgiveness to that part of himself. Then I tried having him imagine a different little boy who had survived similar abuse (I also used this technique with Maria). My hope was that this shift in perspective would lead to a different emotional reaction. It did, and Jason expressed feeling compassion for this other little boy. The next question was how to help him apply this kinder attitude toward himself.

Since a major obstacle for Jason was blaming himself, I wanted to highlight that this hypothetical child was completely blameless. That's why I pointed out there was nothing the child could have done to protect himself. It turned out that this recognition was a lot for Jason to handle, and he started getting hyperaroused (unresponsive, with fast, shallow breathing). I brought his dog into the visualization and we focused on happier thoughts until he was feeling more grounded. At that point, Jason spontaneously said he wanted to tell that little boy the abuse wasn't his fault.

As I mentioned earlier, Piaget (1974) predicts that any child will assume responsibility for whatever happens in his or her life. This is an important insight, but I believe it's not the only reason this pattern is so common for abused children. For many people, there is something comforting about believing that bad things only happen if you do something wrong. It means that it's possible to be completely safe if you can just avoid making any mistakes. The alternative perspective—that bad things can happen no matter what you do—can feel scarier because it admits that you really aren't in control of what happens to you. This is the shift that happened for Jason in that session, and I believe it's why the concepts of blame and blamelessness are so emotionally triggering for him. Realizing that the abuse was not his fault required him to face the harsh reality that a blameless child can be hurt so terribly.

In the last section of the transcript, I guided Jason to picture himself as a 7-year-old together with the other boy and recognize that neither of them is to blame for being abused. This scene was emotionally overwhelming for him at first, so we focused on his dog until he calmed down. When we returned to the image of those two kids, their innocence was immediately obvious to Jason, and he was overcome with compassion.

This case demonstrates the value of practicing a grounding exercise before approaching traumatic memories, how that grounding exercise can be used to regulate emotions during reprocessing, and the role of self-compassion in healing trauma.

ADDICTION

Mindfulness and self-compassion have become extremely popular in the world of addictions treatment. Protocols such as Mindfulness-Based Relapse Prevention (Witkiewitz, Marlatt, & Walker, 2005) are gaining notoriety, and the number of treatment centers that offer basic mindfulness groups is growing rapidly.

I believe the greatest gift mindfulness can offer addictions treatment is a radically different way of understanding and relating to urges. Alcoholics deal with urges to drink, and drug addicts deal with urges to use, but that's not all. Some of our clients deal with urges to self-harm, many people deal with compulsive eating or shopping, and almost every child struggles to control impulsive behaviors of some kind. Teaching methods of coping with and controlling urges is a central part of addictions treatment, and it plays a role in working with many other populations as well.

Most of us believe there are just two options for relating to an urge or impulse: We can act on it or fight against it—submit or rebel. We can let the impulse become our master or make it our enemy. However, mindfulness gives us a third option. It can also become our friend. Through the practice of mindfulness, we learn that we don't have to act on an impulse *or* fight against it. We can just feel it as a sensation in the body.

If we slow down and observe an urge or impulse, we find that it is made out of a distressing sensation in the body coupled with a thought about how to make that distress go away. If an alcoholic were able to slow down enough to observe the urge to drink, he or she would find some kind of somatic distress (maybe agitation and heaviness in the heart) paired with the thought, "Drinking will make this go away." Once the person realizes that urges are nothing more than bodily distress and thoughts, he or she can apply the practices from this book, especially Chapters 4 and 5, to embrace them with open acceptance. The new practitioner slowly builds his or her capacity to tolerate distress and become less reactive when an urge arises. Alan Marlatt, a pioneer in the use of mindfulness with addiction, calls this process "urge surfing." Although it is absolutely essential to help addicts avoid situations and environments that trigger urges, mindfulness gives them a way to strengthen their ability to cope when urges do arise (Ostafin & Marlatt, 2008).

Facing distress is often difficult for addicts, who are in the habit of avoiding discomfort at all costs. In fact, it's possible to view addiction as a pattern of trying to escape from suffering. When we stop this behavior and return to the present moment, we might find a tremendous amount of suffering that has been neglected for

Special Cases • 171

years. The self-compassion practices described in Chapters 6 and 7 can be extremely helpful for healing that suffering.

A great deal of addictions work happens in a group format, and the Dialogue-Based Mindfulness techniques described in this book can be used in groups as well. I generally use a combination of DBM with the more traditional way of leading guided meditations when leading a group. To use DBM in a group, just ask for a volunteer to be guided through a particular practice. The other members get to witness a deeper level of meditation instructions and learn skills they can apply to their own practice. The more traditional way of guiding meditations (in which the therapist speaks to the entire group while they remain silent) can be extremely helpful as well. There are many examples of this latter kind of guided meditation on the Internet.[1]

Finally, learning these practices can be a lot harder for addicts than for many other people, especially outside of an intensive setting. An addict's drug of choice functions as a way to escape distress, requires no effort, and works immediately. Mindfulness and self-compassion, on the other hand, are practices that require considerable effort and might only offer partial relief for a beginner. By contrast, if you are working with a client suffering from social anxiety who has no other way to relieve distress, that person will be highly motivated to practice self-compassion if he experiences even a little relief in his first session. Addicts, on the other hand, are faced with two options for feeling better: the difficult one that requires practice and the easy one that is destroying their lives.

The good news is that with enough practice, mindfulness and self-compassion can become more natural. The more we practice, the more effortless and powerful these skills become, and it is safe to say they can offer much greater relief than any drug if we fully embrace them and make them our new way of life.

PSYCHOSIS

In a recent question-and-answer session, Thich Nhat Hanh was asked how to support someone who struggles with psychosis. He responded, "We must come together as a community and produce a collective energy of mindfulness and compassion to be able to embrace him and help him recover." That's a really different response than the kind most people receive during and after a psychotic episode. Instead, most of them are sent to underfunded and overstretched institutions. Although the staff at these institutions are generally kind-hearted and well-intentioned people, they often struggle with burnout and can have real difficulty empathizing with psychotic symptoms. In this section, I will focus on how we can cultivate our capacity to embrace these clients with mindfulness and compassion, as Thich Nhat Hanh instructs us to do.

I believe that a basic misunderstanding about the nature of psychosis is one of the biggest obstacles to extending compassion toward these clients. Too often they are not seen as people with their own hopes, dreams, and suffering, but rather as diseased brains that have very little in common with "normal people." Thankfully, there is a great deal of research that can help us find our shared humanity and hopefully create relationships that are more beneficial for both therapist and client.

Richard Bentall's book *Madness Explained* (2005) won the British Psychological Society's Book Award and is an indispensible resource for anyone working with people who experience psychosis. In it, Bentall reviews the entire landscape of research into psychosis and uses it to paint a profoundly humanizing and liberating picture. He advocates for a radical shift in how we think about people who suffer from psychosis. The core of his approach is to try to understand and work with the actual complaints or symptoms that these clients bring to us (e.g., hallucinations, delusions, mania), rather than labeling them with a disease. Although I don't review the scientific merit of this model here,[2] I will explain why I believe it has the potential to facilitate a compassionate connection better than thinking in terms of the disease model.

Of the three key ingredients for compassion, it is the third (*We understand that we are not fundamentally separate from each other*) that is most often missing when working with people who experience psychosis. Instead, many therapists view the experience of psychosis as something completely divorced from their own experience.[3] However, research shows that this is actually not true. Oliver Sacks, the celebrated neurologist and author, describes how hallucinations are actually not uncommon and are celebrated by many cultures (2012). Epidemiological studies have estimated that over 10% of all people experience hallucinations at some point in their lives (Bentall, 2005). Deluded thinking is even more common. In fact, I believe anyone who pays close attention to his or her own mind will notice thoughts arise that would be classified as deluded (i.e., bizarre and counter to evidence) according to the DSM.

On the other hand, a full-blown psychotic episode seems to have a quality that separates it from a passing hallucination or delusion. There can be an extreme level of intensity as well as the experience of *losing touch* with consensus reality. However, it is possible to view this situation as the far end of a spectrum rather than as something completely alien to the average person. We have all known pain and loss, but we haven't all experienced PTSD. Yet most therapists don't view the effects of acute trauma as something that is foreign and incomprehensible. It is possible to view psychosis in a similar way. I will now describe a case example of a former client with a history of multiple psychotic episodes that I hope illustrates how this way of thinking can improve our ability to create a compassionate connection.

Psychosis Example: Understanding Jessica

When Jessica was referred to me, she had been out of the hospital just 3 months following her fifth psychotic episode. She was in her mid-30s and living in a special peer-run residential program for people with severe mental illness. She almost never went outside.

Our first sessions were focused on developing a therapeutic alliance. She told me about graphic visions of being tortured during her most recent episode, and I did my best to empathize. She wanted to know if it's possible to experience trauma caused by an event that never actually happened, and I validated how real her hallucinations felt to her. I told her, "If we watch a scary movie, our body gets scared just as if it were really happening. If someone got scared enough at a movie, it could trigger a real trauma response." As we built rapport, Jessica told me more and more about her history with psychosis.

During this phase of treatment, I used two main practices to take care of myself. First, I would send myself compassion whenever I noticed feeling triggered by something she said. I might take a few deep breaths and say to myself, "You wish people didn't suffer like this, and that is a beautiful wish." That kind of thought will often help me let go of any resistance I might feel to what a client is telling me. Second, I would do my best to *personally relate* to her experience, even if it sounded bizarre at first. I was committed to understanding her as a person, rather than a diagnosis.

When we began therapy, Jessica's narrative about psychosis went something like this: "I have a brain disease. A psychotic break can happen without warning for no reason other than the fact that I have schizophrenia." As we developed a detailed history of her life and psychotic episodes, that picture changed. We recognized that there were actually some very predictable triggers. All of her psychotic episodes were preceded by the use of hallucinogenic mushrooms (her first episode) or extreme stress and loneliness (the subsequent four). I commented, "No one can guarantee that these are your only triggers or that you definitely won't have another episode if you steer clear of these. However, it seems like your chance of having another episode would go down significantly if you did." She agreed, and that became an important treatment goal for us. She began to track her stress and loneliness and to reach out to a peer counselor or to me when she needed help coping. Jessica is not unique in this regard. Many researchers have documented how environmental stress predicts psychotic episodes (Norman & Malla, 1993).

Our history taking produced another important insight as well. Jessica had used escaping into fantasy as a primary coping strategy her entire life. When she felt lonely, she would imagine having wonderful friends. When she felt bad about herself, she would imagine having special powers or achieving great accomplishments. I noticed that these fantasies began in a relatively normal fashion and then became increasingly vivid until she could not distinguish fantasy from reality.

I believe we can all identify with using fantasy to cope with stress from time to time. If your boss were to reprimand you, it wouldn't be uncommon to spend some time fantasizing about some form of poetic justice. You might think, "Maybe she'll get caught stealing money or something and everyone will see what a jerk she is. Then maybe they would promote me and I would make sure everyone felt appreciated."

Jessica's most recent psychotic episode began with this kind of fantasizing before it got out of control. She was feeling depressed and responded by isolating herself more and more from other people. She would stay in her bedroom reading poetry by the Sufi poet Rumi, and thinking that if he were still alive, he would be the only person who could possibly understand her. She imagined what kind of man Rumi might have been and kept thinking that they would be soul mates for each other if they ever met. She was completely cut off from other people and spent her days vividly imagining a love affair between her and Rumi. At this point her fantasies took on a life of their own. Her image of Rumi had become more real to her than any actual person in her life. She had lost all awareness that he was imaginary, and she no longer felt in control. Rumi slowly became sadistic, began demeaning her, and eventually torturing her. She was now completely immersed in a psychotic break.

Upon closer inspection, we can see that this episode followed a clear and comprehensible progression. Jessica attempted to use isolation and fantasy to cope with her depression, but these strategies actually made things worse until she reached a breaking point.

Developing this narrative proved to be incredibly therapeutic because it allowed Jessica to predict whether or not she was in danger of another episode, rather than believing they could occur randomly at any moment. If her stress and loneliness were low, she could feel safe. If they were high, she knew to avoid any fantasizing and to reach out to a peer counselor or friend. With this new confidence, she started exercising and took a volunteer job walking dogs at an animal shelter. Two years later, she had a paying job, an apartment, and felt like she had the skills she needed to prevent future episodes.

In working with people who experience psychosis, I've come to believe that this kind of success comes from faith in the possibility that we can understand and personally relate to the client's experience. Months later, as we were discussing different sources of compassion in her life, Jessica told me that my persistence in wanting to understand her was one of the most caring things anyone had ever done for her.

Chapter 10

OVERCOMING COMMON
CLINICAL ROADBLOCKS

This chapter outlines several specific clinical roadblocks to
self-compassion and offers suggestions for how they might be
overcome. If you are looking for general help developing comfort
and confidence using self-compassion in psychotherapy, there
are two practices that I recommend. In Chapter 4, I described a
way to practice with the transcripts in this book by covering the
text with a piece of paper and revealing just one line at a time.
You pause and reflect on each line until you feel really confident
that you understand *why* I said what I said or *why* the client
reacted the way that he or she did. I believe this method can be
an extremely helpful learning tool. Second, and more impor-
tantly, I recommend applying the practices in this book to your
own life and your own suffering. The next chapter will be
entirely focused on this. It can also be helpful to seek consulta-
tion or training from someone who is more experienced in this
way of working. See www.timdesmond.net for training oppor-
tunities and resources.

SPECIFIC ROADBLOCKS

In this section I present some common roadblocks to clinical effi-
cacy in question and answer format.

Can I Personally Relate to My Client's Experience?

It can be difficult to guide someone through a problem that
doesn't make sense to you. Therefore, putting yourself in your client's shoes can help a lot. Imagine saying or doing whatever your
client says or does. Now ask yourself if it feels foreign and irrational, or if you can relate. Do you really understand *why* your client
would say or do that? What would you have to feel or believe to
act the same way if you were in similar circumstances? If you
aren't sure, keep asking the client questions until it makes sense.
Some therapists are afraid to persist in asking questions because
they don't want the client to feel pestered or misunderstood. You
can transparently express your simple desire to understand the
client's experience as accurately as possible by saying something
like, "I just want to make sure I really understand you so I can be
as helpful as possible."

Is There an Alliance around Goals?

Imagine asking your client, "What are your goals or hopes for
therapy?" What would he or she say? If the answer is clear, identifies a realistic goal, and you feel supportive of that goal, then you
have an alliance around goals. If not, I strongly recommend focusing on this area before proceeding to specific interventions.

Motivational Interviewing is an excellent tool for connecting
with a client's goals. It guides you to identify and empathize with
the client's internal motivation for change. For example, you
might ask your client, "How would you like your life to be different?" In response, some clients will name something they would
like to change about themselves, such as being less angry. This
makes for a straightforward therapy goal.

Other clients, however, will say they want someone or something outside of themselves to change. That external goal might be realistic or it might be completely out of their control. Examples of a realistic external goal could be getting released from your program or no longer getting arrested for drunk driving. The task here is to help the client identify what kind of personal change would be needed to accomplish that goal. For example, to be released from your program, the client might have to convince the staff that he or she has developed sufficient emotional control, so "emotional control" can become the goal for therapy.

It can be harder to create an alliance with clients who name an external change that isn't possible or is outside of their control. For example, a client could want to be exempt from the rules of your program, have unrealistic demands for other people to change, or want to change something that happened in the past. In this situation, it can be helpful to ask, "If that doesn't (or can't) change, what strength or skill would you need to develop to make it more tolerable?" If a client wants his mother to stop getting angry with him, that might not be realistic (especially if the mother gets angry with everyone). However, you might be able to help him see that his mother's anger wouldn't hurt him so much if he could develop more self-compassion.

Finally, some clients will try to convince you that no positive change is possible. In this situation, it is important to pay close attention to the client's nonverbal communications. If the client seems exhausted and defeated while saying nothing will help, some empathy and encouragement can go a long way. It is possible this client has tried to change and failed many times. It might be helpful to say, "I know you've tried a lot of different things that haven't helped, but I believe there is a chance we could find something that will help if we keep trying." On the other hand, if the client seems defiant or even proud of being a hopeless case, you are likely dealing with self-sabotage, which is covered in Chapter 8.

Is There an Alliance around the Treatment Plan?

Does your treatment plan come directly from your client's goals? Assuming you have created a strong alliance around goals, think about how the interventions you plan to use pertain directly to those goals and be willing to explain this connection to your client.

Does your client seem to doubt that the interventions you are using will help? If so, explain your thinking to the client and have a frank conversation about how they make sense to you. You can use honest statements such as, "I can't guarantee this will help, but I think there is a good chance it will. Would you like to try and see?" You can also explicitly ask, "Is there any other way of approaching this problem that would make more sense to you?"

Do I Feel Strong Positive Regard and Compassion for My Client?

If you picture your client right now, what feelings arise in your body? Do you feel warmth and openness, or tension and aversion? Do you feel blank and distant? One of the best predictors of effective therapy is the therapist's experience of strong and unambivalent positive emotions toward the client. Whenever these feelings are *not* present, however, it's important not to criticize ourselves, but to recognize how we feel and send ourselves compassion. The next chapter discusses this point in more depth.

Is the Client Trying to Please Me?

If you believe your client is telling you that a practice is more effective than it really is, there are two important points to communicate to them. First, it is extremely helpful to know when a practice isn't working so you can move on to a different one. There are countless ways to practice, and you want to try different ones until you find something that helps. Second, mindfulness is about learning to tolerate strong feelings, not about trying to make them go away.

Are There Problems Using the Practice Outside of Therapy?

Some clients might benefit from mindfulness and self-compassion in session with you, but not be able to use those practices in their daily lives. You've found a way of practicing that helps them, but they aren't using it when it matters. For example, you might have helped a client to use mindfulness of the body to dramatically reduce her anxiety, but she never uses that practice on her own. When this is the case, it could be a problem with diligence or it could be a form of self-sabotage. The next two sections explore problems involving a lack of diligence, since self-sabotage has already been covered.

Does the Client Intellectually Appreciate the Importance of Practice?

Many people don't fully appreciate the necessity of diligent practice. Instead, they believe it is possible to learn a new skill in session with you, not think about it for several weeks, and then be able to remember it in a moment of crisis. However, we know that the only skills we can access in moments of crisis are the ones that have become automatic habits. The analogy of learning self-defense can be helpful to explain how this works. If you want to learn self-defense, you have to practice it over and over until it becomes automatic. Only then will you be able to use it effectively if you are ever attacked. Make sure your client realizes the need to practice mindfulness and self-compassion on a regular basis so that those skills will be available in a moment of crisis.

Does the Client Have Enough System 2 Energy to Practice Effectively?

Learn about the circumstances of your client's life and pay special attention to anything that could deplete their System 2 energy. Look for major stressors, overwork, and sleep issues. If your client doesn't have enough System 2 energy to practice new skills, you shouldn't expect a lot of progress. Instead, you can explore whether it might be possible to help your client eliminate major stressors or work on relaxation.

Is Jargon Creating Obstacles?

If your client seems to have an aversion to the terms *mindfulness, meditation*, or *compassion*, you can just stop using them. Some highly religious people can be afraid that meditation conflicts with their faith. If you work with clients like this, you might want to do some research about how silent contemplation is taught in their tradition. Remember, all we are doing is trying to help our clients develop beneficial states of mind. When describing mindfulness, you can say, "Some people find that when they stop fighting against their negative feelings, those feelings actually go away. I'm not sure if that will happen to you, but we can try." When describing self-compassion, you can say, "Your brain has a circuit that scientists call the *Care Circuit*. It is active when you are feeling warmth and love. If we can develop ways to activate that circuit, it can have powerful effects on improving your mood."

Are There Potential Medical or Lifestyle Problems?

Serious mental health symptoms can be caused by medical issues such as a tumor or thyroid problem, dietary issues such as vitamin deficiency or excess caffeine, and lifestyle issues like lack of exercise or social connection. It just takes a minute to learn whether your client has had a recent medical checkup and if there are obvious dietary or lifestyle issues. You should also assess for major stressors such as losing a job or the death of a family member. You can find a thorough review of dietary and lifestyle interventions at www.timdesmond.net.

Are There Other Sources of Resistance or Unexplained Difficulties?

If your client is not responding well to therapy and you can't understand why, review Chapter 8 on self-sabotage.

Chapter 11

SELF-COMPASSION PRACTICES FOR THE THERAPIST

In 2005, I was living in Plum Village, Thich Nhat Hanh's monastery in southern France, and I heard him give a talk about a banana tree. He had been asked a question about the meaning of life by one of his students, and responded by telling a story about a deep insight he experienced while meditating in the jungle in Vietnam many years earlier.

He said he was sitting by the foot of a young banana tree and contemplating its leaves. It had just three leaves. One was fully grown, broad and flat and dark green. The second leaf was still partially curled up beneath the first, and the third leaf was very light green and tender, just beginning to unfurl. Looking deeply, he saw that the eldest leaf was fully enjoying her life as a leaf. She was absorbing the sun and rain, radiating beauty and peacefulness. However, she had not abandoned the other leaves to pursue her own happiness. In fact, as she nourished herself, basking in the sunshine, she was also nourishing the younger leaves, the banana tree, and the entire jungle. He went on to explain that human beings are just like this leaf. As we nourish ourselves with peacefulness and compassion, we are also supporting the well-being of every other living thing.

Let's take a moment to reflect on this image. Imagine yourself as this beautiful, fully grown banana leaf. Recognize that, although you are unique, you are also deeply connected to the rest of the tree and to the whole jungle. The more you nourish yourself with the sunshine of serenity and self-love, the more those energies are available to support everyone and everything to which you are connected. Try to see that the greatest gift you can give the world is your own peacefulness and happiness.

NOURISHING OUR OWN HAPPINESS

When we recognize the incredible value of our own happiness, we become determined to do whatever we can to nourish it. We want to care for it as if it were our only child. We want to give it every possible condition to support its growth. This deep motivation to cultivate our own well-being is essential for the development of self-compassion. We begin by truly giving ourselves permission to be happy. We have to see that it is possible to prioritize our own well-being *as a service to others*, rather than as a way of neglecting them. As Thich Nhat Hanh would say, our happiness is not separate from the happiness of other people. In fact, our happiness *is the happiness of other people.*[1]

Once we feel a strong motivation to cultivate our own peace and freedom for the sake of all beings, the next step is learning how to come home to the present moment. Many of us spend our entire lives rushing to get somewhere else, and one of the greatest gifts we can give ourselves is the permission to stop and rest. Our rushing arises from agitation, fear, and the belief that life is not OK as it is. We need to change something, fix something, or solve some problem in order for happiness to be possible. Only then will we allow ourselves to stop. We are driven by our habit to achieve or just to keep busy. We might even be afraid of what thoughts or feelings would arise if we slowed down enough to listen to ourselves.

However, if we look deeply, we can realize that happiness is already possible in this moment. In fact, this very moment is the only place that happiness can ever be found, because all of life happens in the present moment. Thich Nhat Hanh often says that in every moment of life, there are infinite reasons to be happy and infinite reasons to suffer. What matters is where we focus our attention. If you were to take a few minutes and make a list of everything you *could* be upset about right now, it would be easy to create a long list. On the other hand, if you were to spend the same amount of time making a list of everything you *could* be happy about—the blue sky, the laughter of children, your loved ones—that would be a pretty long list too. Paying attention to the conditions for happiness that are already present can lead to the experience of profound gratitude.

To some people, this might sound naïve. Does focusing on the positive mean that we passively accept unsafe or unjust situations? Does it mean that we should never try to make our lives better or make the world a better place? It absolutely does not. Thich Nhat Hanh is an example of someone who has worked tirelessly for peace, sustainability, and to share the teachings of mindfulness with people around the world. When we recognize that happiness is always available, we begin to act from a more grounded and peaceful place instead of being frantic and anxious. Our actions become even more effective because we can see any situation more clearly, and we don't waste our precious energy worrying.

Peace Is Every Step

It is possible to learn how to sit, walk, and breathe in a way that makes happiness and peace available in every moment of life. When Thich Nhat Hanh was first ordained as a Buddhist monk in 1942 in Vietnam, he was given a small book of poems. He was told to learn them all by heart so he could recite them throughout the day. There was a poem for waking up, one for putting on his robes, one for washing his face, and so on. This was his introduction to Buddhist monastic training. The poems were reminders to bring mindfulness and compassion to every action and every moment of life. He has adapted these poems for contemporary use in his book *Present Moment, Wonderful Moment* (Hanh, 1990). This is the poem for waking up:

> Waking up this morning, I smile.
> Twenty-four brand new hours are before me.
> I vow to live fully in each moment,
> and look at all beings with the eyes of compassion. (p. 3)

Imagine approaching every moment of life in this way. You wake up filled with gratitude and wonder at the miracle of being alive. As you sit up in bed, you are deeply aware of all the sensations in your body. You enjoy the feeling of the soft sheets and blankets, and you notice the pleasant temperature on your skin. You pause and take 10 or 12 conscious breaths, completely unhurried and smiling broadly that you have clean air and functioning lungs. As you shower, you fully enjoy the experience of showering. As you eat breakfast, you bring your complete concentrated presence to every bite of food and savor the taste and texture. You feel overwhelmed with gratitude for having enough food to eat. Every action and every moment of life becomes a miracle.

This practice is also possible when life brings you challenges. As you drive to work in heavy traffic, you can enjoy your breathing and the feeling of relaxation in your body. You might also feel grateful for the teachers and practices that help you to be happy in that moment. When you look at the clock and see that you are already 10 minutes late, you could think, "I'm moving as quickly as I can, and I will arrive whenever I arrive." You don't feel rushed at all. In fact, you might begin to say to yourself, "I am arriving fully in every moment, exactly where I am." When you do arrive at work, you are refreshed and radiating joy. Later, as you fill out huge stacks of paperwork, you are breathing with mindfulness and aware of the privilege to be able to earn a living while helping people in need.

THE SPIRIT OF EXPERIMENTATION

Although it is possible to enjoy every moment of life, it's not easy for most of us. We have to experiment with many different ways of practicing to learn what works best for us in different moments. For example, if I'm late for an appointment, I will ask myself if there is anything else I could do to arrive sooner. If there is a practical and realistic solution to the problem, I want to do that. However, there might be nothing more I can do. If I'm stuck in traffic, surrounded by cars that aren't moving, I don't have the power to change the situation in that moment. Recognizing this, I remind myself to practice letting go of my attachment to being on time and try to consciously cultivate helpful thoughts like, "There is nothing more you can do right now. You can just let yourself enjoy your breath."

If these thoughts don't seem to be helping me feel better, I might switch to mindfulness of the body. Noticing any tension or agitation, I allow myself to feel all the sensations in my body without trying to make them change. Often, this leads to calming down and feeling more spacious. However, if I feel overwhelmed by the strength of my distress in that moment, I might switch to a self-compassion meditation—for example, putting a hand on my heart and saying to myself: "You would really like to be on time because you want to respect other people, and that is a wonderful value. You don't have the power to make that happen right now, even though you would like to. You are suffering because you can't have what you want, which happens to everyone. May you know that all of your thoughts and feelings reveal your beautiful human nature."

I believe this process of experimenting with different practices is a lot like choosing the right medicine for a certain illness. Imagine having a huge medicine cabinet with hundreds of types of medicines, herbs, and homeopathic remedies. If you were feeling unwell, it would be up to *you* to choose which medicine to take. If you chose well, you would feel better. If you chose poorly, you might feel worse. Now imagine that you chose a medicine that made you feel worse. However, instead of saying, "Oops, I should stop taking this and try something else," you decided to keep taking more and more of it and eventually concluded, "I guess medicine can't help this problem."

This is how many people treat meditation. There are hundreds of forms of meditation that are available to us, but many people only bother to learn one. If it doesn't help them in a particular situation, they think, "I guess *meditation* can't help this." In reality, we can try different forms of practice until we find one that helps.[2] It is our responsibility to figure out how to use different practices in ways that benefit us.

To give you a better picture of how to experiment with different practices, I'll share a couple more specific examples from my own life. If I'm waiting in line at an airport and notice that I'm feeling bored, I will often come back to my breath. However, I won't just space out or try to dull my mind. Instead, I'll use the breath as a reminder to come back into the present moment and ask myself, "Where are you? What is happening right now? Is there anything you need to be happy that you don't already have?" This practice helps me to recognize that everything I need to be happy is already present right now. The only thing that was missing was my *awareness*.

When I'm feeling anxious, I will always start by coming back to the sensations in my body. I take a few mindful breaths and allow myself to feel whatever tension is there. Sometimes just connecting with my body in this way is enough to create a lot of relief, but other times distressing thoughts will persist.

When that happens, I find that it's important to balance accepting my negative thoughts with telling myself that things are going to be OK. It's delicate and requires practice. I want to be careful not to fight against or resist any distressing thoughts, but I also want to encourage myself to notice that I'm safe in the present moment.

I might consciously think, "No matter what happens now, you are safe and you'll be OK." However, just a moment later the thought "I can't let this happen—I have to find a way to stop it" might arise in my mind on its own. It's important not to fight this thought. Instead, I recognize that it's just a thought and say, "There's a part of me that really doesn't want this to happen, but I know I'll be OK no matter what." It's a dialectical process, in which we contextualize negative thoughts rather than fighting with them.

PRIORITIZING SELF-CARE

In our work we are exposed to a huge amount of other people's pain. Over time, being present with all this pain can deplete our energy, and we may even develop secondary trauma symptoms. The summer before I began graduate school in psychology, I was on a long meditation retreat and asked one of the elder monks about this issue. I said, "How can I keep from getting overwhelmed by other people's suffering without shutting down emotionally?"

He was quiet for a while and then responded: "It begins by recognizing the importance of caring for yourself. You have to recognize suffering when it is present in you, and know that caring for that suffering is the most important thing you can do. Don't let anything else come first. Breathe with your suffering and embrace it with compassion. Don't stop until you feel light and calm in your body, even if it takes hours."

Not many of us demonstrate this kind of dedication to self-care. In fact, many mental health professionals will prioritize almost every other responsibility over nourishing their own well-being. I know it's not easy, but we have to recognize that caring for ourselves is the greatest gift we can give to the world.

The Two Faces of Self-Care: Cultivating Happiness and Healing Suffering

Self-care has two main elements: cultivating happiness and healing suffering. If we focus too much on one and ignore the other, we end up out of balance. Thich Nhat Hanh teaches that we need to nourish our peace and joy in order to have enough energy to be fully present with suffering.

He uses the term "psychic circulation" to describe how we alternate back and forth between cultivating happiness and embracing our suffering. Poor psychic circulation can come from trying to ignore our suffering through distracting ourselves with TV, Internet, alcohol, or anything else. When we avoid our suffering, it festers and grows until it becomes so strong that it's impossible to ignore. Poor psychic circulation can also come from being so focused on grief or anger or sadness that we forget to replenish our reservoir of peace and happiness. In that case, it is like running out of the fuel we need to effectively transform suffering.

As I mentioned in Chapter 9, our mindfulness and happiness must be strong enough to embrace our suffering for the practice to be effective. Buddhist psychology teaches that our positive emotions have to be big enough and strong enough to contain our suffering (Hanh, 2001). When we get in touch with some psychological pain, if we can fully embrace it with mindfulness and compassion, the result is healing. However, every time we bring up suffering and are unable to surround it with positive emotions, the suffering gets worse.

Compassion Fatigue and Burnout

Our positive emotions are like a fuel that allows us to remain fully present in the face of suffering. If we run out of fuel, we don't have the energy to care for ourselves or anyone else. This is why it is so important to learn how to cultivate peace and happiness in the present moment. Many of us get to a point in our careers when we hit a wall. We've been giving so much to others and neglecting ourselves for so long that we don't have any energy left to give. This is called *compassion fatigue* or *burnout*.

Even if you are not currently feeling burned out, it is never too early to start paying attention to replenishing the energy that you give to others. Many of us don't even notice we are feeling depleted until we get to a point that we can no longer function. It is like someone who doesn't look at the fuel gauge on their car until they press the gas petal and the car doesn't move. We don't notice that our store of happiness and compassion is getting low until we are completely exhausted or emotionally shut down.

The first step in preventing compassion fatigue is using mindfulness to notice when our reservoir of positive emotions is running low. We want to replenish ourselves long before we are completely exhausted. Second, we recognize the value of nourishing our own happiness, and we prioritize self-care in our lives. Finally, we learn how to skillfully and efficiently cultivate happiness in the present moment through being mindful of the positive elements in life, connecting with other people, practicing kindness toward ourselves and others, and letting go of all of the things in life that distract us from what is truly important. We will explore developing a plan for your own self-care later in this chapter.

WORKING WITH DIFFICULT CLIENTS

Take a moment and picture your toughest client. You can choose someone whose personality gets under your skin, whose intensity can feel overwhelming, or whose symptoms don't seem to be improving from therapy. Let the image be really clear in your mind. Let yourself see that person's facial expressions and hear how he or she talks with you. Is he or she angry, dissociated, pleading, or something else?

Now keep that image there and notice all of the sensations in your body. Bring your awareness to any tension, heaviness, or other sensation that might arise. Name whatever you are feeling in your body. It might be tension in your jaw, agitation in your legs, or a strong impulse to move in some way.

Do your best to stay focused on the sensations in the body. Even if it's really uncomfortable, try to let yourself *feel all of it* and not lose yourself in discursive thinking. If a strong thought arises, notice that it is just a thought. Don't argue with it or agree with it. Just accept it and allow it to be there. You can say, "This thought came up in my mind. It can stay or go, however it wants."

Stay with the image of your client and keep coming back to the physical sensations in your body. Let those sensations be as powerful as they want to be. Let them get stronger, stay the same, or change in any other way. Experiment with saying to yourself, "It's OK to feel this," or "I'm strong enough to tolerate this," or "These feelings are welcome." You might even imagine holding these feelings with the tenderness of a mother holding her crying baby.

You might naturally discover some part of yourself that is in need of compassion. Experiment with different ways of directing compassion to yourself until you find one that feels powerfully helpful. You might try the following:

- Put your hand on your heart and imagine sending healing energy to yourself.
- Picture some other being (someone you've known, a religious figure, etc.) sending compassion right to the place where your suffering is located in your body.
- Say phrases to yourself such as: "May you be happy. May you be healthy. May you be safe. May you be loved."
- Picture yourself when you were a child and express love and compassion toward your younger self.

If you haven't done so already, take at least 10 minutes to try this practice. If it takes an hour or more before you begin to feel peaceful and solid, continue to persist. If you notice that you feel stuck or blocked in any way, experiment with different forms of practicing until you find something that helps. With enough determination, you will find something that works for you.

Once you have finished with this exercise, picture your client again. Notice how your feelings have changed. Can you relate to this client differently from a more peaceful state of mind? Many therapists find that practicing self-compassion opens up new possibilities for working with tough clients.

OBSTACLES TO SELF-CARE

Once you appreciate the tremendous value of your own well-being, you want to make sure that you are doing everything you can to nourish it. It is like a precious jewel that you want to keep safe. However, there are a lot of things that can get in the way of prioritizing self-care.

If we don't understand what truly causes happiness, we might think we need a lot of money or career success to be happy. However, positive psychology research has shown that this viewpoint isn't true (Diener, 2009). Imagine looking at the file of a research subject that says she is wealthy and professionally successful. From that information, could you predict whether she is happy? Of course not. However, if you had no information about her finances but she had scored very high in measures of optimism and self-compassion, then it is likely she would also report a lot of well-being.

If we believe career success is more important than cultivating self-compassion, we will direct more of our time and energy toward that goal. Sometimes I wonder what a society would look like if everyone actually put more time and energy into cultivating compassion and gratitude than in trying to improve their material circumstances. Research suggests we'd be much happier (Diener, 2009).

Another major obstacle to self-care is the pressure we put on ourselves to constantly care for others at the expense of our own needs. We feel so responsible to meet other people's needs that we can neglect our own and eventually become exhausted. This is why it is so important to recognize that our well-being is not separate from the well-being of anyone else. We can see that our own happiness is like the fuel we need in order to help others.

Finally, it is not possible to adequately care for ourselves if we habitually fill up every free moment with distractions like TV, Internet, alcohol, etc. If we let go of these distractions, we can rediscover some of the time and space we need for self-care.

INTEGRATING SELF-COMPASSION PRACTICE INTO YOUR LIFE

Now let's focus on creating an ongoing self-compassion practice that fits your priorities and your life. As you consider the vast possibilities of different ways to practice, remember that every little bit helps. If you can practice mindfulness and self-compassion for just 5 minutes every morning when you wake up or every evening before bed, that can lead to real benefits. However, you should also remember that the more time and energy you invest in your practice, the greater the results you will find. Five minutes is good, 2 hours is better, and all day long is ideal.

It can be helpful to articulate what matters most to you. If your family is your top priority, ask yourself what could be a greater gift to them than becoming a more fully present and compassionate person. If you value being of service to others or seizing the day and enjoying life, reflect on the same question: "What could be more important than developing self-compassion in my life?" Please spend a few minutes contemplating this question.

If you conclude that developing self-compassion would be one of the greatest uses of your precious time and energy, the next step is to think about putting that value into practice. What would your life look like if you really made self-compassion one of your top priorities? Imagine what it would be like if you invested as much time and energy into cultivating this virtue as you put into some of the other important areas of your life. Again, please pause for a few minutes and really reflect on this question.

Four Forms of Practice

With all of the countless forms of practice that are available, it can be somewhat overwhelming to decide what to prioritize in your own life. I will review four major categories of practices as a way to reflect on what might be the best fit for you. I recommend experimenting with different forms until you find at least one that you like from each category.

Retreats

There are hundreds of retreat centers and monasteries in the United States that offer a huge range of programs. This kind of intensive, immersion experience can be one of the best ways to deepen your meditation practice. It can also be an excellent first step for someone who is just starting to practice meditation. Sometimes sitting for 20 minutes on your own, or even an hour in a group, can be difficult for beginners because it's hard to settle into a practice. However, after a few days on retreat, even a complete beginner will often have a deep-enough experience that it can become the foundation for their daily practice at home.

When deciding what kind of retreat to try, there are many considerations. Obviously, location and finances are important to most of us. There are more retreat centers in the Northeast and West Coast compared to many other areas of the country, so people who live in other areas might decide they want to travel to find a place that feels right. There is also a huge range of costs for retreats, from Goenka-style Vipassana retreats[3] that are completely free of charge (you are asked to make a voluntary donation only after you've completed a course) to spa-like centers that charge up to $1,000/day or more.

Then you might consider whether you want to go to a center that is Christian, Buddhist, secular, or another tradition. Would you prefer a center that is run by a staff of laypeople[4] or monastics[5]? Do you want a solo retreat experience where you are alone in a cabin all day (many retreat centers offer this option), or would you prefer participating in a structured retreat schedule with others? Would you like a retreat that is totally silent (the Goenka-style retreats mentioned above involve 10 days in total silence in a group), or would you prefer some periods of silence as well as time to connect with others?

Personally, I prefer retreats at Plum Village and related monasteries for a couple reasons. Foremost, the opportunity to be in the presence of Thich Nhat Hanh and listen to his teachings is truly incredible. If there are teachers that you admire, there is nothing like practicing alongside them. I recommend familiarizing yourself with teachers such as the Dalai Lama, Pema Chödrön, Jack Kornfield, Tara Brach, Sharon Salzberg, and Ajahn Amaro. If you can attend a retreat with a master teacher, that would be extremely fortunate.

Another benefit of Plum Village retreats is that the monks and nuns who lead them also live at the monasteries year-round and have dedicated their entire lives to developing mindfulness and compassion. They have taken vows of poverty and chastity in order to devote all of their energy to practice. These retreats are like temporarily joining a living community of people who have integrated mindfulness into every aspect of their lives.

Finally, Plum Village-style retreats are not merely focused on silent sitting meditation. Instead, you are encouraged to treat every moment of the day as a form of meditation. This includes formal practices of sitting and chanting, as well as walking, listening to teachings, small-group discussion, and eating. For me, the focus on bringing mindfulness to many different kinds of activities helps me to more fully integrate the practice into my daily life. However, it also requires significant self-discipline. With less formal structure than some other retreats, you must rely on your own diligence to treat every moment as a meditation. It is very different than the highly structured Goenka-style retreats or a *sesshin* at a Soto Zen center, in which you might practice silent sitting for 10 hours a day.

There are many wonderful retreat centers in every part of the United States. I recommend experimenting with different kinds of retreats until you find one that you like, and then doing your best to spend at least a few days on retreat every year. When I joined the Order of Interbeing, a collective of dedicated practitioners founded by Thich Nhat Hanh, I made a commitment to spend at least 60 days each year on retreat. That equates to one full day of practice each week and two 5-day retreats a year. Whenever possible, I try to spend long periods of time studying with Thich Nhat Hanh in Plum Village.

Bells of Mindfulness

Another important element of practice is integrating mindfulness and compassion into our daily lives when we aren't on retreat. Thich Nhat Hanh recommends finding ways to stop and come back to our practice as often as possible. I covered this topic in Chapter 2, as well as earlier in this chapter, so I will be brief here.

Choose at least one daily activity to perform mindfully. It could be eating a meal in silence or going for a mindful walk. There are many ways to practice walking meditation, but the one that Thich Nhat Hanh teaches most often is to practice arriving in the present moment with each step. Usually we walk in order to arrive at some destination. However, it's possible to feel truly satisfied and at home in every moment of walking.

If you have 5 or 10 minutes between clients, that can be a great time to send yourself compassion. If there is some particularly stressful part of your day, try to integrate mindfulness and compassion into that activity, and see if you can recognize that all of the conditions needed for happiness are still available, even then.

The Support of a Community

The Sanskrit word for community, *sangha*, is often used to describe groups of people who come together to practice mindfulness and compassion.[6] Practicing in a community makes everything so much easier. If you try to practice alone, you must rely on your own willpower to avoid getting carried away by negative habits. However, a group of like-minded people can provide a kind of collective inertia that helps you live in harmony with your values. If you sit down to meditate on your own, you might get bored or distracted and get up after five minutes. On the other hand, you might find that sitting for twenty minutes or more is easy in a group.

Thich Nhat Hanh strongly emphasizes coming together to practice in community. He uses the image of a drop of water that lands on the top of a mountain to illustrate this point. If that drop wants to succeed in making it all the way down the mountain and into the ocean, it will need to be carried by a river. If it tries to go alone, it will surely dry up. He says that we can create communities of practice to "go as a river" and support each other toward our goals.

Therapists can form special communities of practice to support each other. They can practice sitting and walking meditation, listen to a dharma talk, and share how they are using mindfulness and compassion practices in their work and lives.

Just after getting married, my wife and I left our jobs and many good friends in California to move across the country to New Hampshire in order to live at a residential mindfulness community. Morning Sun Mindfulness Center, where we live now, is a retreat center that is based in a residential community of dedicated practitioners, much like a monastery. However, the residents are all laypeople, with families and jobs, who have committed themselves to prioritizing the practice of mindfulness and compassion. I can't express how incredibly supportive it is to live with people who share these values and practice together.

Formal Daily Practice

A formal daily practice can be a powerful anchor in your life. It is the time you set aside each morning or evening for explicitly cultivating mindfulness and compassion. Formal practices can include sitting meditation, walking meditation, prayer, chanting, studying spiritual or inspirational texts, tai chi, yoga, and listening to the sound of a bell. When you study teachings, do so in a contemplative manner. Reflect deeply on what you read and seek to apply the teachings to your life, rather than just trying to accumulate knowledge.

Experiment with different types of practices in order to discover what works best for you. Thich Nhat Hanh has a book called *Chanting from the Heart: Buddhist Ceremonies and Daily Practices* (2006) that describes many different kinds of formal practice. There are so many varieties of meditation that I believe there is something out there for everyone. If you haven't yet found one that you enjoy, keep looking. You will.

If you would like to incorporate self-compassion meditation into your daily practice, you can experiment with something like this: Sit in a comfortable position with your eyes open or closed. You might want to sit in a chair or on a cushion on the floor. Many people find that sitting with an erect spine helps them to feel more alert.

Begin by bringing your attention to the sensation of your breathing. Try to follow the physical sensation of your breath coming in and going out from the beginning until the end of each breath. Take several breaths in this way as you bring your mind back in touch with your body in the present moment. Allow yourself to enjoy the sensation of your breath and recognize that it is a pleasant sensation.

After a period of focusing on your breathing, begin to direct compassion toward yourself in the present moment. Scan your body and mind for any discomfort. If there is any physical tension or emotional distress, direct compassion right at its source. Continue sending compassion to yourself, and specifically to your suffering, until you can no longer find any distress in your mind or body. Finally, spend a few minutes just savoring this deep experience of wellness.

CONCLUSION

Recent research suggests that nearly 20% of Americans suffer from some kind of serious mental health problem (National Institute of Mental Health, 2014). In other words, our society is suffering deeply and in desperate need of more compassion.

In Buddhism, the concept of Bodhicitta (pronounced Bodhichitta) describes a deep aspiration to relieve suffering and create well-being for oneself and others. Although this aspiration can be hidden underneath layers of fear and ignorance, I believe that it is present in every person.

We are fortunate as mental health professionals because our work is in harmony with our Bodhicitta. We are blessed with the privilege of earning a living by helping others. Let's not forget how lucky we are.

I hope that this book has supported you in some way. May you continue to grow and develop as a source of compassion in the world. May you help others become sources of compassion for themselves. May you be happy. May you be healthy. May you be safe. May you be loved.

References

Allione, T. (2008). *Feeding your demons: Ancient wisdom for resolving inner conflict.* Hachette Digital.

Baumeister, R. F., Campbell, J. D., Krueger, J. I., & Vohs, K. D. (2003). Does high self-esteem cause better performance, interpersonal success, happiness, or healthier lifestyles? *Psychological Science in the Public Interest, 4*(1), 1–44.

Baumeister, R. F., Smart, L., & Boden, J. M. (1996). Relation of threatened egotism to violence and aggression: The dark side of high self-esteem. *Psychological review, 103*(1), 5.

Bennion, L. L. (1959). *Religion and the pursuit of truth.* Salt Lake City, UT: Deseret Book.

Bentall, R. (2005). *Madness explained: Psychosis and human nature.* New York, NY: Penguin.

Breines, J. G., & Chen, S. (2012). Self-compassion increases self-improvement motivation. *Personality and Social Psychology Bulletin, 38*(9), 1133–1143.

Breines, J. G., Thoma, M. V., Gianferante, D., Hanlin, L., Chen, X., & Rohleder, N. (2014). Self-compassion as a predictor of interleukin-6 response to acute psychosocial stress. *Brain, Behavior, and Immunity, 37,* 109–114.

Burgdorf, J., & Panksepp, J. (2006). The neurobiology of positive emotions. *Neuroscience & Biobehavioral Reviews, 30*(2), 173–187.

Chödrön, P. (2010, September). Tonglen: Bad in, good out. *Shambhala Sun,* 58.

Davidson, R. J. (2012). *The emotional life of your brain: How its unique patterns affect the way you think, feel, and live—and how you can change them.* New York, NY: Penguin.

Dȩbiec, J., Doyère, V., Nader, K., & LeDoux, J. E. (2006). Directly reactivated, but not indirectly reactivated, memories undergo reconsolidation in the amygdala. *Proceedings of the National Academy of Sciences of the United States of America, 103*(9), 3428–3433.

Dickerson, F. B., & Lehman, A. F. (2011). Evidence-based psychotherapy for schizophrenia: 2011 update. *Journal of Nervous and Mental Disease, 199*(8), 520–526.

Diener, E. (Ed.). (2009). *The science of well-being: The collected works of Ed Diener* (pp. 11–58). New York: Springer.

Flückiger, C., Del Re, A. C., Wampold, B. E., Symonds, D., & Horvath, A. O. (2012). How central is the alliance in psychotherapy?: A multilevel longitudinal meta-analysis. *Journal of Counseling Psychology, 59*(1), 10-17.

Fodor, J. A. (1983). *The modularity of mind: An essay on faculty psychology.* Cambridge, MA: MIT press.

Frankl, V. E. (1961). *Man's search for meaning.* New York, NY: Simon & Schuster.

Fredrickson, B. L. (1998). What good are positive emotions? *Review of General Psychology, 2*(3), 300-319.

Fredrickson, B. L. (2013). *Love 2.0.* New York, NY: Hudson Street Press.

Gazzaniga, M. (2012). *Who's in charge?: Free will and the science of the brain.* London: Constable & Robinson.

Germer, C. K. (2009). *The mindful path to self-compassion: Freeing yourself from destructive thoughts and emotions.* New York, NY: Guilford Press.

Gilbert, D. (2009). *Stumbling on happiness.* New York, NY: Random House.

Goetz, J. L., Keltner, D., & Simon-Thomas, E. (2010). Compassion: An evolutionary analysis and empirical review. *Psychological Bulletin, 136*(3), 351-374.

Hanh, T. N. (1990). *Present moment, wonderful moment.* Berkeley, CA: Parallax Press.

Hanh, T. N. (1996). *Cultivating the mind of love: The practice of looking deeply in the Mahayana Buddhist tradition.* Berkeley, CA: Parallax Press.

Hanh, T. N. (1998). *The heart of the Buddha's teaching: Transforming suffering into peace, joy & liberation: The four noble truths, the noble eightfold path, and other basic Buddhist teachings.* New York, NY: Random House.

Hanh, T. N. (2001). *Transformation at the base: Fifty verses on the nature of consciousness.* Berkeley, CA: Parallax Press.

Hanh, T. N. (2006). *Chanting from the heart: Buddhist ceremonies and daily practices.* Berkeley, CA: Parallax Press.

Hanh, T. N. (2009). *The blooming of a lotus: Guided meditation for achieving the miracle of mindfulness.* Boston, MA: Beacon Press.

Hanh, T. N. (2011). *Anger: Buddhist wisdom for cooling the flames.* New York, NY: Random House.

Hanh, T. N. (2013a). *The path of emancipation: Talks from a 21-day mindfulness retreat.* Berkeley, CA: Parallax Press.

Hanh, T. N. (2013b). *Under the rose apple tree.* Berkeley, CA: Parallax Press.

Harris, S. (2014). *Waking up: A guide to spirituality without religion.* New York, NY: Simon & Schuster.

Harter, S. (1993). Causes and consequences of low self-esteem in children and adolescents. In *Self-esteem* (pp. 87–116). New York, NY: Springer.

Hayes, S. C. (2004). Acceptance and commitment therapy, relational frame theory, and the third wave of behavioral and cognitive therapies. *Behavior Therapy, 35*(4), 639–665.

HH Dalai Lama XIV, (1995). The Power of Compassion. India: Harper Collins.

HH Dalai Lama XIV, (2006). *Kindness, clarity, and insight.* Ithaca, NY: Snow Lion.

Hofmann, S. G., Grossman, P., & Hinton, D. E. (2011). Loving-kindness and compassion meditation: Potential for psychological interventions. *Clinical Psychology Review, 31*(7), 1126–1132.

Hupbach, A., Gomez, R., Hardt, O., & Nadel, L. (2007). Reconsolidation of episodic memories: A subtle reminder triggers integration of new information. *Learning & Memory, 14*(1–2), 47–53.

Kabat-Zinn, J. (2003). Mindfulness-based interventions in context: Past, present, and future. *Clinical Psychology: Science and Practice, 10*(2), 144–156.

Kahneman, D. (2011). *Thinking, fast and slow.* New York, NY: Macmillan.

Kahneman, D., & Beatty, J. (1966). Pupil diameter and load on memory. *Science, 154*(3756), 1583–1585.

Kahneman, D., & Deaton, A. (2010). High income improves evaluation of life but not emotional well-being. *Proceedings of the National Academy of Sciences, 107*(38), 16489–16493.

Kegan, R., & Lahey, L. L. (2001). The real reason people won't change. *Harvard Business Review. 79(10).* 84-91.

Kernis, M. H. (1993). The roles of stability and level of self-esteem in psychological functioning. In Baumeister, R. (ed.), *Self-esteem* (pp. 167–182). New York, NY: Springer.

King, M. L. (1957). Loving Your Enemies. *Christmas Sermon.* Lecture conducted from Dexter Avenue Baptist Church, Montgomery, AL.

Krieger, T., Altenstein, D., Baettig, I., Doerig, N., & Holtforth, M. (2013). Self-compassion in depression: Associations with depressive symptoms, rumination, and avoidance in depressed outpatients. *Behavior Therapy, 44*(3) 501–513.

Kristeller, J. L., & Johnson, T. (2005). Cultivating loving kindness: A two-stage model of the effects of meditation on empathy, compassion, and altruism. *Zygon®, 40*(2), 391–408.

Kross, E., Bruehlman-Senecal, E., Park, J., Burson, A., Dougherty, A., Shablack, H., . . . & Ayduk, O. (2014). Self-talk as a regulatory mechanism: How you do it matters. *Journal of Personality and Social Psychology, 106*(2), 304-324.

Lacasse, J. R., & Leo, J. (2005). Serotonin and depression: A disconnect between the advertisements and the scientific literature. *PLoS Medicine, 2*(12), e392.

Leary, M. R., Tate, E. B., Adams, C. E., Batts Allen, A., & Hancock, J. (2007). Self-compassion and reactions to unpleasant self-relevant events: The implications of treating oneself kindly. *Journal of Personality and Social Psychology, 92*(5), 887-904.

Lind, L. (1991). Thanatos: The drive without a name: The development of the concept of the death drive in Freud's writings. *Scandinavian Psychoanalytic Review, 14*(1), 60–80.

Lutz, A., Brefczynski-Lewis, J., Johnstone, T., & Davidson, R. J. (2008). Regulation of the neural circuitry of emotion by compassion meditation: Effects of meditative expertise. *PloS One, 3*(3), e1897.

Lutz, A., Greischar, L. L., Rawlings, N. B., Ricard, M., & Davidson, R. J. (2004). Long-term meditators self-induce high-amplitude gamma synchrony during mental practice. *Proceedings of the National Academy of Sciences of the United States of America, 101*(46), 16369–16373.

Monfils, M. H., Cowansage, K. K., Klann, E., & LeDoux, J. E. (2009). Extinction–reconsolidation boundaries: Key to persistent attenuation of fear memories. *Science, 324*(5929), 951–955.

Montgomery, R. W. (1993). The ancient origins of cognitive therapy: The reemergence of Stoicism. *Journal of Cognitive Psychotherapy, 7*(1), 5–19.

Nader, K., Schafe, G. E., & LeDoux, J. E. (2000). Reply–reconsolidation: The labile nature of consolidation theory. *Nature Reviews Neuroscience, 1*(3), 216–219.

National Institute of Mental Health. (2014). *Prevalence of any mental illness among adults.* Retrieved from http://www.nimh.nih.gov/health/statistics/prevalence/any-mental-illness-ami-among-adults.shtml.

Neff, K. D. (2003). Self-compassion: An alternative conceptualization of a healthy attitude toward oneself. *Self and Identity, 2*(2), 85–101.

Neff, K. D. (2011). *Self-compassion: The proven power of being kind to yourself.* New York, NY: William Morrow.

Neff, K. D., & Germer, C. K. (2013). A pilot study and randomized controlled trial of the mindful self-compassion program. *Journal of Clinical Psychology, 69*(1), 28–44.

Neff, K. D., Hsieh, Y. P., & Dejitterat, K. (2005). Self-compassion, achievement goals, and coping with academic failure. *Self and Identity, 4*(3), 263–287.

Neff, K. D., Kirkpatrick, K. L., & Rude, S. S. (2007). Self-compassion and adaptive psychological functioning. *Journal of Research in Personality, 41*(1), 139–154.

Neff, K. D., & McGehee, P. (2010). Self-compassion and psychological resilience among adolescents and young adults. *Self and Identity, 9*(3), 225–240.

Neff, K. D., & Vonk, R. (2009). Self-compassion versus global self-esteem: Two different ways of relating to oneself. *Journal of personality, 77*(1), 23–50.

Neimeyer, R. A. (2006). Re-storying loss: Fostering growth in the posttraumatic narrative. In Calhoun, L., & Tedeschi, R., (Eds.), *The handbook of posttraumatic growth* (68-80). New York, NY: Routledge.

Nelson, E. E., & Panksepp, J. (1998). Brain substrates of infant–mother attachment: Contributions of opioids, oxytocin, and norepinephrine. *Neuroscience & Biobehavioral Reviews, 22*(3), 437–452.

Nelson, S. K., Fuller, J. A., Choi, I., & Lyubomirsky, S. (2014). Beyond self-protection self-affirmation benefits hedonic and eudaimonic well-being. *Personality and Social Psychology Bulletin, 40(8)*, 998-1011.

Norman, R. M., & Malla, A. K. (1993). Stressful life events and schizophrenia. I: A review of the research. *British Journal of Psychiatry, 162*(2), 161–166.

Olendzki, A. (2008). The real practice of mindfulness. *Buddhadharma: The Practitioner's Quarterly, 7*, 50–57.

Ostafin, B., & Marlatt, A. (2008). Surfing the urge: Experiential acceptance moderates the relation between automatic alcohol motivation and hazardous drinking. *Journal of Social and Clinical Psychology, 27(4),* 404-418.

Panksepp, J. (1998). *Affective neuroscience: The foundations of human and animal emotions.* Oxford, UK: Oxford University Press.

Panksepp, J., & Biven, L. (2012). *The archaeology of mind: Neuroevolutionary origins of human emotions.* New York, NY: Norton.

Panksepp, J., Siviy, S. M., & Normansell, L. A. (1985). Brain opioids and social emotions. In Reite, M., (Ed.), *The psychobiology of attachment and separation* (pp. 3–49). Waltham, MA: Academic Press.

Piaget, J. (1974). *Understanding causality* (D. & M. Miles, Trans.). New York, NY: Norton.

Plesser, H. E., Eppler, J. M., Morrison, A., Diesmann, M., & Gewaltig, M. O. (2007). Efficient parallel simulation of large-scale neuronal networks on clusters of multiprocessor computers. In *Euro-Par 2007 Lecture Notes in Parallel Processing* (pp. 672–681). Berlin/Heidelberg: Springer.

Pollak, S. M., Pedulla, T., & Siegel, R. D. (2014). *Sitting together: Essential skills for mindfulness-based psychotherapy.* New York, NY: Guilford Press.

Rogers, C. R. (1957). The necessary and sufficient conditions of therapeutic personality change. *Journal of Consulting Psychology, 21(2),* 95-103.

Rothschild, B. (2000). *The body remembers: The psychophysiology of trauma and trauma treatment.* New York, NY: Norton.

Rumelhart, D. E., McClelland, J. L., & PDP Research Group. (1995). *Parallel distributed processing, vol. 1: Foundations.* Cambridge, MA: MIT Press.

Sacks, O. F. (2012). *Hallucinations.* New York, NY: Knopf.

Samuels, R. (2000). Massively modular minds: Evolutionary psychology and cognitive architecture. In Carruthers, P., & Chamberlain, A. (Eds.), *Evolution and the human mind: Modularity, language and meta-cognition* (pp. 13–46). Cambridge, UK: Cambridge University Press.

Schiller, D., Monfils, M. H., Raio, C. M., Johnson, D. C., LeDoux, J. E., & Phelps, E. A. (2009). Preventing the return of fear in humans using reconsolidation update mechanisms. *Nature, 463(7277),* 49–53.

Siegel, D. J. (2001). Toward an interpersonal neurobiology of the developing mind: Attachment relationships,"mindsight," and neural integration. *Infant Mental Health Journal, 22*(1–2), 67–94.

Sparks, J. A., Duncan, B. L., & Miller, S. D. (2008). Common factors in psychotherapy. In Lebow, J. (Ed.), *Twenty-first century psychotherapies: Contemporary approaches to theory and practice* (pp. 453–497). New York, NY: Wiley.

Tobias, B. A., Kihlstrom, J. F., & Schacter, D. L. (1992). Emotion and implicit memory. In Christianson, S. (Ed.), *The handbook of emotion and memory: Research and theory* (pp. 67–92). New York, NY: Psychology Press.

Vaillant, G. E. (1977). *Adaptation to life.* Cambridge, MA: Harvard University Press.

Valenstein, E. (2005). *The war of the soups and the sparks.* New York, NY: Columbia University Press.

Wampold, B. E. (2013). *The great psychotherapy debate: Models, methods, and findings* (Vol. 9). New York, NY: Routledge.

Weng, H. Y., Fox, A. S., Shackman, A. J., Stodola, D. E., Caldwell, J. Z., Olson, M. C., . . . & Davidson, R. J. (2013). Compassion training alters altruism and neural responses to suffering. *Psychological Science, 24*(7), 1171–1180.

Westbury, C. (2012). *How fast?* Retrieved from https://www.ualberta.ca/~chrisw/howfast.html.

Whitaker, R. (2001). *Mad in America.* New York, NY: Basic Books.

Witkiewitz, K., Marlatt, G. A., & Walker, D. (2005). Mindfulness-based relapse prevention for alcohol and substance use disorders. *Journal of Cognitive Psychotherapy, 19*(3), 211–228.

Wyatt, W. J., & Midkiff, D. M. (2006). Biological psychiatry: A practice in search of a science. *Behavior and Social Issues, 15*(2), 132–151.

End Notes

Chapter 1

1   These three key ingredients are a way of restating the traditional Four Noble Truths of Buddhism. Thich Nhat Hanh translates those as (1) suffering exists; (2) suffering has causes; (3) well-being exists; (4) well-being has causes.

2   Kross (2014) and colleagues found that self-talk can be more powerful when we address ourselves using second-person or third-person pronouns, rather than the first person.

Chapter 2

1   It is certainly possible that some other contemplatives or other people who haven't been tested could show greater levels of happiness than these monks did. If they achieved this profound well-being through a different practice, then that would be an important finding. However, at the time of this writing, no research subjects have demonstrated greater happiness markers than the monks in Davidson's study.

2   Although no one refutes Panksepp's core claim that these are the primary affective brain circuits, other scientists conceptualize "basic emotions" differently. See Boucher and Brandt, 1981; Ekman, 1999; Izard, 1977; Roseman, Spindel, and Jose, 1990; C. A. Smith and Ellsworth, 1985; Tomkins, 1984.

3   There is debate about the precise nature of causation between neuronal activation and neurotransmitters/cytokines/hormones. See Valenstein's (2005) work for more detail. What is clear is that behaviors can activate this system, which includes neural circuits and neurotransmitters.

4   Likely in the hippocampus.

5   Even the best therapists don't help 100%, which gives us permis-

210 • End Notes

sion to recognize those instances and help the client move on. Duncan (see Sparks et al., 2008) calls it "failing successfully."

Chapter 3

1 Buddhist psychology stresses the centrality of compassion to transform negative emotions.

Chapter 4

1 Andrew Olendzki (2008) translates these wholesome factors as: equanimity, non-greed, non-hatred, self-respect, respect for others, faith, tranquility, lightness, malleability, wieldiness, proficiency, non-rectitude, and the absence of the opposite of those final six factors.
2 In Theravada Buddhism this is taught through the doctrine of *dependent arising*. In Mahayana Buddhism, it is taught through the doctrine of *emptiness*.
3 Right View is explained in more detail in the Foundations of Self-Compassion training; see www.timdesmond.net.

Chapter 6

1 A more literal translation is *divine abodes*, but traditional commentaries also describe the word *Brahma* as meaning "limitless." The word *Vihara* refers to these qualities as being a place of refuge for the mind to dwell, but they are clearly a list of virtues.
2 I consider the field of "character education" as a separate field of study. I am specifically referring to research in the domain of psychology, especially relating to clinical work.
3 I believe that *tonglen* could be used clinically, but it is not my expertise.
4 Instructions for developing *karuna* are different and begin by picturing the most miserable and unfortunate person possible.
5 I don't necessarily take this report literally. It could be that his current distress makes him unable to remember more recent experiences of feeling OK.
6 This is a clue that he might equate being pure with being lovable.

Chapter 7

1 This concept is chiefly advocated by proponents of connectionism, massive modularity, and distributed agency in cognitive science. I'm avoiding the level of detail at which this theory is debated in the hope of presenting something that most major theorists could

accept. Certainly, a basic amount of distributed agency is undeniable, based on split-brain studies and the localization of certain competencies in the brain (see Harris, 2014, for a review). When Fodor (1983) argues that higher functions are not modular, I believe he is using the term more specifically.

2 In computer science, *parallel processing* means that the various processes are fully independent. Some theorists argue that the term is not the best metaphor for the brain's processing architecture. However, *distributed processing* is a more general term that allows for interconnected but relatively autonomous processing. That description clearly applies. Many cognitive scientists and neuroscientists have adopted *parallel distributed processing* as a term to describe the functioning of the brain. For those who are familiar with computer science, I believe that *multi-agent system* is the closest model for brain functioning from that discipline.

3 Not perfectly, but harmonious enough to allow us to function.

4 I agree with many of the core concepts of internal family systems, such as the indeterminate number of psychological parts that interact and desire well-being for the person. However, I prefer to emphasize the idiosyncratic nature of these parts and their role in constructing multiple narratives, rather than fitting them into descriptive categories.

Chapter 8

1 I'm describing some of the more simplistic schools of cognitive–behaviorism.

2 These are the more theoretically robust schools of cognitive–behaviorism.

3 For a more technical description of modular constructivism, see www.timdesmond.net.

4 Some constructivists would prefer the phrase "construct meaning" to "create stories," but that's a level of detail I don't think is necessary to make my point. It can also obscure how dual process theory in cognitive science refers to the same story-creating tendency.

5 They can both access core cognitive abilities, such as simple perception, language, etc., so there is some indirect connection.

6 There are certainly more than two parts in Larry's mind and more than two stories. However, we are interested in these two in particular because of their impact on his mental health. The younger part that believes he is bad is causing a lot of suffering, and the more mature part is asking for my help as a therapist.

Although we don't know for sure, some neuroscientists esti-
mate that the brain makes about 20 *million billion* calculations
(that's *16* zeros) each second (Westbury, 2012). In fact, a few
years ago, scientists used the fourth largest supercomputer in the
world to simulate the amount of calculations a brain performs in
1 second. With about 83,000 extremely fast processors running
in parallel, it took 40 minutes to complete what the brain does in
1 second (Plesser, Eppler, Morrison, Diesmann, & Gewaltig,
2007). Given the fact that a neuron is several million times
slower than a modern computer processor, the number of different processes in the brain is at least in the billions. I certainly
could not create a model for how these billions of processes structure our mental experience. I'm just hoping to explain how therapists can benefit from being aware that separate parts create
separate stories, especially when trying to work with stubborn
self-criticism and self-sabotage.

7   See Gestalt, Focusing, Hakomi, Emotionally-Focused Therapy,
    etc.
8   This is assuming those parts have remained implicit and not been
    integrated into more mature identity.

Chapter 9

1   There are examples on www.timdesmond.net, and many free,
    guided meditations by Thich Nhat Hanh, Sharon Salzberg, Jack
    Kornfield, Tara Brach, and Chris Germer on other sites.
2   Bentall makes a convincing argument that modern diagnostic
    categories are not the most scientifically rigorous way to think
    about psychosis. This perspective was recently echoed by none
    other than Thomas Insel, the director of the National Institute of
    Mental Health. See http://www.nimh.nih.gov/about/director/
    2013/transforming-diagnosis.shtml.
3   Another important obstacle to empathy for psychotic clients is
    overmedication. Many neuroleptics have powerful side effects,
    including sedation and confusion. In fact, Dickerson and Lehman
    (2011) report that although psychotherapy was found to be effec-
    tive for psychosis in the 1950s and 1990s, several studies found no
    efficacy in the 1960s through 1980s, which was the peak of Hal-
    dol use. I believe Haldol created such a stupor that therapy became
    ineffective. Although second-generation neuroleptics are better,
    they are far from ideal. See Whitaker (2001) for more.

Chapter 11

1   I'm certainly not saying that our happiness is more important than other people's. According to Buddhist psychology, there is just no fundamental difference between one's own happiness and the happiness of others. One can't be more important because no one is separate. When we are happier, we support the happiness of others. When we contribute to the happiness of others, that makes us happy as well.

2   Even a practice like mindfulness of breathing doesn't help every situation and can even be harmful in the wrong context. If you try to ignore your feelings by focusing on your breath, this would obviously create more suffering in the long term.

3   See www.dhamma.org.

4   For example: Spirit Rock Meditation Center, Insight Meditation Society, and Omega Institute.

5   For example: Plum Village, Deer Park, and Blue Cliff Monasteries.

6   Some traditions use the word *satsang*, which means "true community" or "community of truth."

Index

Note: Italicized page locators indicate figures; tables are noted with *t*.

external goals, 179

eye-movement desensitization and reprocessing (EMDR), 67

 relaxation techniques and, 165

 self-compassion practices integrated with, 162

fairness, maintaining, self-criticism, and, 154

faith, 210n

fantasies, psychotic episodes and, 174–75

Fear Circuit, in brain, 22

Feeding Your Demon process, 159

feeling tone, 81

fight-flight-freeze response, 67

 Fear Circuit in brain and, 22

 during therapy, retraumatization and, 162

financial pressures, as obstacles to self-care, 193

finger pointing at the moon, Buddha's teachings likened to, 60–61

fMRI. see functional magnetic resonance imaging (fMRI)

forgiveness, bringing to younger abused self, 168

formal daily practice, 198–99

Four Limitless Virtues, 95–97

Four Noble Truths of Buddhism, three key ingredients and restatement of, 209n

Frankl, V., 164

Fredrickson, B., 95, 98

French-Vietnamese war, 161

Freud, S., 134

friend(s)

 compassion and transformation of enemies into, 153

 turning inner critic from enemy into, 138–41, 146

 urges or impulses treated as, 170

functional magnetic resonance imaging (fMRI), 20, 21

Gazzaniga, M., 30

generosity, 59

Germer, C., 2, 37, 133, 212n

Gestalt interventions, self-sabotage work and, 159

Gilbert, D., 38, 39, 40

goals

 alliance around, 110, 112, 178–79

 clarifying, 53